THE LONGEST RUN

By Rainer Hertrich
with Devon O'Neil

Copyright © Rainer Hertrich
November 2015
Copper Mountain, Colorado

No portion of this book may be reproduced in part or in full without the written consent of Rainer Hertrich or Devon O'Neil

For more information, visit www.thelongestrunbook.com

I

It was a Tuesday — January 10, 2012 — when my life unraveled like a ball of twine rolling downhill.

The second week of the year is always one of the winter's coldest at Copper Mountain, Colorado, where I have lived for 33 years, but I'd dealt with much colder days than that one. (If you've never felt your eyeballs start to freeze, you're missing out!)

The day before, as I bent over to buckle my ski boots, I could barely reach them. I felt bloated like a walrus from head to toe. My lower legs had turned into cankles, with no way to tell where the calf ended and the ankle began. My belly was hanging over my waist like a boiling pot of cheese. The pants I wore Monday no longer fit me on Tuesday. Even if I could have reached the buckles on my boots, my feet wouldn't fit in them. I had no idea what was going on. My boots didn't just shrink overnight.

All of this came on the heels of a strange pattern that had developed over the weekend. After skiing every day for eight years, two months, and nine days — by far the longest consecutive-days ski streak by any human being on record — I suddenly couldn't catch my breath halfway down the mountain. I was panting like a bitch in heat. I spend multiple hours per day above 11,000 feet elevation, where oxygen is scarce, but this was different. Normally I can ski top-to-bottom runs for six hours straight, and when I get to the bottom after each run I can talk to people right away. Now, even my legs were getting sore on the way down, which simply doesn't happen. The snow was hard and fast, so it wasn't like I was skiing powder and getting worked by the uneven snow. Not knowing what is wrong with your body is one of the scariest feelings in the world. All I knew was that something was seriously wrong.

Monday night, I decided to get myself checked out by a doctor. So the next morning, before the flood of ski-injury victims inevitably hit the Copper clinic, I left my one-bedroom condo at the base of the resort and made the three-minute drive to the other side of the village.

Inside, once I got settled, different nurses came and went, everyone loosely diagnosing what they thought the problem might be. No one seemed to know for sure. Finally, after three hours in limbo, they took me into a room and X-rayed my chest. A doctor came to see me after that. His expression was serious, the kind of look you never want to see from someone who just read your chest X-rays.

"Your heart's swollen on one side," he said. "There's something going on. You need to take an ambulance to the hospital and go see a cardiologist — now."

His words hit me like an uppercut. I didn't know what to do. The doctor was well aware of my world-record ski streak — and that if I didn't ski, it would be over. Hell, everyone at Copper knew. I'd been on CNN and in newspapers and magazines around the world: the crazy snowcat driver who follows an endless winter, skiing in the northern hemisphere for 10 months a year and the southern hemisphere for the other two. I hadn't missed a day since George W. Bush was in his first term as president.

I took a deep breath and told the doctor I had never been a good listener, and that, well, no offense, but I had to go skiing. "Just in case you misdiagnosed me, I'm going to do one really easy run," I said, almost apologetically but firm nonetheless. "That way, at least I'll have the day taken care of and the streak will be alive."

The doctor shook his head. I could tell that he did not approve. He looked me in the eye and tried once more to convince me not to go skiing. "You could die, Rainer. I'm not just saying that." (My name, for the record, is pronounced "Rye-ner.")

As strange as this sounds now, back then, in that moment, with my proudest achievement hanging in the balance, I was willing to risk my life for my streak without a second thought.

I thanked him and promised that I would drive right to the hospital after I took one run. From the clinic I went home to my condo, almost shaking with fear. I threw on my boots, grabbed my skis, and boogied over to the American Eagle chairlift as fast as I could.

They kept me so long at the clinic that I already was cutting it close to my 2 o'clock appointment at the hospital. Then a pair of tourists fell off the chairlift at the bottom and it stopped, with me just two towers up from the base. It was 1:40. I called my mom from the lift and told her about my chest X-ray. She lives in Frisco, a neighboring ski town six miles down Ten Mile Canyon from Copper. She agreed to come pick me up for my appointment.

My mind was swirling by the time I finally reached the top of the mountain. Was I about to die? Was my ski streak really worth all this stress? I linked seven low-angle trails to ski back to my condo, rushing while trying to stay calm. My mom was holding the front door open when I got there. "Come on, Rainer!" she shouted. "We have to go!"

I ripped off my skis and boots, threw them in my living room, and jumped in the car.

At the hospital, the cardiologist, Dr. Warren Johnson, looked at my cardiograph and said very calmly, "You've got some problems, but we'll just take you into the ER and let those doctors check you out so we're all on the same page."

I was about to walk to the emergency room when Dr. Johnson stopped me. Someone brought a wheelchair instead. I wondered what the hell was so wrong that they didn't want me to walk 150 feet?

They rolled me into the ER like an invalid, strapped me down on an exam bed and started taking my blood pressure as well as a dozen other readings. Very methodical, very businesslike … and haunting if you are the man strapped to the gurney. Then Dr. Johnson and the other two ER docs went out into the hall and had a pow-wow. When they came back, one of them said, "We all agree you need to go up to the ICU and that's all there is to it. You could die if you don't."

In the intensive care unit, they put me on a different bed and conducted a full-body CT scan, where they run you into a tube that spins around. From there, it was up to the ICU and into a room that would become my home for the next three days, strapped down with tubes and IVs running in and out of me, constantly taking injections and eating pills, a most deplorable end to the happiest time of my life.

I had an irregular heartbeat, or atrial flutter in doctor's terms. One chamber of my heart was flapping like a wounded duck, and it just happened to be the chamber that sends water through your bloodstream so that every part of your body stays hydrated. Since it was beating so fast, the chamber wasn't actually pumping any blood and was cavitating, which is why the water was flowing into any cavity it could find. It was flooding my gut, my chest, and, especially, thanks to gravity, my legs.

When I last weighed myself, a few months prior, the scale read 220 pounds. When they weighed me in the ICU, I was 265.

I lay in the hospital that first day, crushed, wishing for a miracle. I knew I had until midnight Wednesday to keep the streak alive.

Nothing changed, however.

On Wednesday afternoon, I began making some of the most painful phone calls I've ever made.

"It's over," I said. This wild, weird, one-of-a-kind adventure that began on November 1, 2003, and took me from Colorado to Utah, Idaho, Oregon, Chile, and Argentina every year for most of my 40s … has come and gone. I reached one friend while he was halfway through a bottle of tequila, in the midst of a ski trip in interior British Columbia. He was even more stunned than I was.

I fell one week short of skiing 3,000 consecutive days. The previous high number on record was 365, set by a British ski journalist and his French girlfriend in 1994. Even more painful, I finished 2 million vertical feet shy of 100 million, a goal I'd been aiming for since the streak began.

People asked me whether I was more devastated by my near-death heart condition or by the end of the streak. I'd say it was even. I was terrified for my health; I knew that January 10 could have been my last day on this planet. But I was just as bummed that the streak was over, especially the way it ended. A broken leg, torn knee ligament — I'd understand that a lot better. But no one ever expects his heart to stop working at age 50.

When I told people it was over, I was pretty much in tears, quivering, sadder than I'd ever been. It was horrible. The next day, I e-mailed friends and supporters around the world and told them about my broken, fluttering heart. It hurt to type the news, but the number of well wishes I got in return made me smile. It surprised me how much I'd impacted people's lives simply by going skiing every day.

During my three miserable days in the ICU I did a lot of soul searching and praying to God, because I was still in a tenuous state. The worst part was trying to sleep. I've had sleep apnea for my whole life. This did not sit well with the nurses whose job it was to keep me alive. Whenever you stop breathing in the ICU, you trigger an alarm and the nurses come rushing in like linebackers to wake you up. The first time it happened, they shouted: "You completely stopped breathing!" And I said, "Yeah, I do that during the day too, and I'm aware of it when I do." I guess my body just thinks it has enough oxygen, so it doesn't need to breathe for a while.

I slept 12 hours my first day out of the hospital and stayed at my mom's house for a month. She cooked for me and took care of me like I was a little boy again. I was stuck to the oxygen machine and couldn't do much else.

I wasn't out of the woods by any stretch, either. I had to stay away from salty foods, drink a lot of water, take my blood pressure twice a day and my medication religiously. I was basically a vegetable, lying on the couch like a dying dog, watching it dump snow outside after it had been dry all winter.

The one thing that kept me motivated during that demoralizing month was the pursuit of 100 million vertical feet, which I'd hoped to hit within 100 months and should have occurred on "Leap Day," or February 29, 2012. (People brag about hitting 1 million vertical feet in a year; my high was 13.5 million.)

To stay on a pace of 1 million feet per month, I had to average 33,000 vertical feet per day — no small task even for a fit skier. (I called it going to work in my vertical office.) But keeping the daily ski streak alive was simple. I only had one rule for a day to count: Put your skis on and ski.

I skied through bruised ribs, separated shoulders, frostbite that turned my skin white and blue, and the everyday aches and creaks that can make a 50-year-old body protest like a wailing newborn when the wind chill is minus-50 degrees Fahrenheit and it's time to go skiing.

One day in Argentina, I skied 106 runs on a high-alpine T-bar in the pouring rain. Another day in Colorado, I skied for 12 hours straight, from 9 a.m. to 9 p.m. If the lifts were closed, I either hiked up the mountain or skied down from the top of an alpine pass and hitchhiked back up. I spent multiple summers camped in a tent on public land to keep my costs down.

People always asked if I was going through a midlife crisis, but it was the only way I wanted to live. I spent $80,000 of my own money to support the streak, and sacrificed much of what society considers a normal life. I missed holidays and birthdays and funerals. I eventually drove away my girlfriend, Ginger, because she kept asking me to prioritize her over skiing, and I just couldn't.

I was adamant about doing what I was doing and absolutely nothing was going to get in the way. Except for my own death, which almost happened.

A lot of people disagreed with the way I ran my life, but as I often told friends and family, "I ain't gonna get rich, but I sure am happy!"

The 100-million-foot goal took priority late in my streak. I didn't broadcast it, but in the back of my mind I figured if I were ever going to quit the streak and get on with my life, that number would be a good place to end. When my heart started acting up I was so close I could taste the celebratory Crown Royal and Cokes. It was two months away, if that; basically a hummingbird's wing flap in the grand scheme of things.

After my arrhythmia was diagnosed, I spent 40 days off snow. Instead of slaughtering vertical, as I did on my big days, I fought my insurance company, which was trying to say my heart problem was a pre-existing condition and they weren't liable for $105,000 in medical bills. Nice try, douchebags!

I took a trip to the ocean to clear my head and put my toes in the sand, a sensation I'd been missing for nearly a decade. But my feet were still so mangled from my ski streak that I never actually took my shoes off.

In late February, I moved home to Copper and the doctors finally cleared me to ski again. My streak was dead, but I decided I was going to hit the dang 100 million no matter what. So I skied as hard as I could for 45 days straight, zoning out the rest of the world just as I had the previous eight years.

I hit the magic number on a snowy April day — Friday the 13th — at Copper Mountain. I was still crushed that my streak had ended beyond my control. I cried on the chairlift the moment I thought about it. But passing 100 million vertical feet finally gave me the peace I needed to let my body rest and heal. After I passed that number, I didn't ski for five months.

The Hertrich family as pictured in 1966. Clockwise from top: My dad, Fred; my brother, Greg; me; my sister, Angela; and my mom, Gisela. I was 5.

II

Aside from my family and friends, nothing has done more to make me who I am than skiing.

I was born in Düsseldorf, West Germany (back then, in 1961, there was still an East and a West), and grew up mostly in Estes Park, Colorado, a small mountain town at the gateway to Rocky Mountain National Park. I was the oldest of three children.

My dad, Friedrich Hertrich — Fred — was a computer engineer before anyone knew what a computer was. He moved to America to find work shortly after I was born. He started in Oregon, where his brother lived, and eventually landed a job with IBM, which was based in Silicon Valley, California. I spent my first year living at the Bear Springs Ranger Station, 20 miles east of Timberline Lodge in Oregon. I lived with my Uncle Adolf and Aunt Gabrielle, who met in grade school in Bavaria, north of Munich, and emigrated from Germany in 1953.

After four years in San Jose, Dad got transferred to Colorado, which proved mighty fortuitous for young me. We packed up our Pontiac station wagon and relocated to Ski Country USA in 1965.

We lived in Boulder at first, before it became a breeding ground for yuppies. Some university professor vanished to Central America and we moved into his house. There was a bomb shelter in the backyard; my other backyard was Flagstaff Mountain.

My dad was a mechanical genius of sorts — he designed and wrote the code for one of the first cassette-drive computers. The cherry-wood prototype, which sat on his desk for years, always reminded me of his accomplishment. But the best trait he handed down to me was his love of sliding down mountains on planks. He was a skier, and a devoted one.

He took me skiing shortly after we got to Colorado. We'd hop in the car and drive up to Loveland, Ski Idlewild (a 400-foot hill that closed in 1986), Winter Park, Eldora, Vail, and Hidden Valley, among others. Because my younger brother, Greg, and baby sister, Angela, were too little to ski, it was usually just me and my dad for the first few years. My mom would stay home and take care of my siblings while we ripped powder turns.

My dad was a patient teacher until I started beating him down the hill. He didn't like that. He was always waiting and looking for me, because he thought I'd be behind him. Like any kid, it brought me great satisfaction to ski faster than my dad.

My parents divorced when I was 7. My dad was bummed out, I was bummed out, and my mom was bummed out, but she didn't want to live with a man who was always working. He often didn't come home from the office until 3 or 4 in the morning.

She moved us up to Estes Park when I was 10, in 1971. This was most important because Hidden Valley Ski Area was in Estes. The snowy pitches became my sanctuary. Officially, Hidden Valley opened in 1955, but locals skied its trails long before then. Lift tickets were cheap — about $5 for a day pass — and the scene was pure adventure for kids like us. I fell in love with the place immediately.

We had a couple of next-door neighbors who were lift operators at the ski area, so we'd get up early and catch a ride with them every morning that we didn't have to go to school. We'd help them dig out and pack the lift maze first thing, and as soon as the lift was running and their safeties were checked, they'd let us on the hill. All the ski patrollers knew us so they didn't mind.

There were other privileges too. At the start of every season, we helped build a tow line to open the upper lifts, which got us dibs on first T-bar for the winter and made us heroes among our friends. Jumping was technically not allowed, but if we wanted shovels to go build jumps, they'd give us shovels to build our jumps. We'd just hide them behind a snow drift — out of sight, out of mind — to appease management. We were like a little Rat Pack, always around and up to something.

I stuck my first front flip on snow when I was 13, the first kid in our school to do one. This was back in the early days of hot dogging. A lot of my friends were into throwing 360s, but for whatever reason, the spinning tricks didn't click for me. The day I landed my front flip, we carved a lip into a drift with a nice steep landing at Hidden Valley. Ski patrol knew we were there, but if the boss happened to go up that day, he never would have seen it.

Once we got into high school, we tried to get a race team going within the school. But because the previous team hadn't behaved very well, the administrators had a bad taste in their mouths and didn't want anything to do with us. So my friend Phil Wagner and I came up with a different idea. We knew an instructor who'd been a racer, Greg Hurt, and thought he might be open to coaching us. We ran into him at a stoplight on Main Street in Estes, and we pitched our team to him. We had enough kids interested that he pretty much agreed on the spot.

We called ourselves the Estes Park Race Club — EPRC. One of the moms knit us all matching stocking caps, red with a fluffy yellow ball on the end. Then we got jerseys with "EPRC" and our names printed on the arm. I actually sewed some foam pads into my forearms because we were banging hard bamboo gates and needed protection; this was long before breakaway gates came about.

As the team progressed, we took on something of an outlaw identity. We showed up to races wearing blue jeans and our jerseys; when we walked around Vail, Breckenridge, and Winter Park — all these fancy ski areas whose teams had matching padded speed suits — people would look at us funny, like, Who are you guys? Where's Hidden Valley? Where's Estes Park? But the thing was, we kicked ass. We'd take three or four positions in the top five, and then another two in the top 10. That was average.

We didn't have much grooming at Hidden Valley, so we were all used to skiing backcountry conditions — basically crud and windblown shit — which meant we could ski fast in most conditions. We were tough little bastards; we weren't afraid of anything, really. I think that's why we did so well in our meets. Ironically, the high school caught wind of this because we were in the newspaper all the time. Our football team was sucky and our wrestling team was worse, but the race team was always front and center because we crushed our opponents. Of course the school asked us to join them, but we declined. "You had your chance," we told them.

That may have caused some problems for me with the high school later on. I worked really hard my senior year so I could graduate a semester early and race and train every day the rest of the year. Well, lo and behold, right before I was going to finish my last class, they said I was missing an eighth credit of sophomore vocation. (That was due to wrecking my mom's car before I had a driver's license, so I was forced to take driver's ed, which was at the same time as sophomore vocation. I made up for that by going to a vocational school to learn carpentry.)

The high school told me that they wouldn't graduate me and that I had to be in school every period for the rest of the year. Really, the way I remember it, all they wanted was a body count, because that's how they got their funding.

I was furious with them. I basically flipped off the superintendent, the principal, and the counselor and said, "I'll see you when I turn 18. I'll come back and take the GED." I did just that and aced every category in the test. So at least I knew that I knew something. But my dad was livid with me for quitting high school and not going to college. As time went on and I worked at ski areas then started consulting internationally with just my high school education, his disappointment wore off and he got over the fact that I didn't grow up as he engineered me to be. By the time he died in 1999, I think he had even become proud of me for following my own path. But it took many years.

Instead of going to high school, I ran gates every day. I'd set my own courses, and if they started getting rutty, I'd move the course, slip in my old ruts, and start running gates again. Everyone at Hidden Valley supported that. It wasn't like they closed the trails down. I still had to ski with the tourists and guests. But for the most part, there wasn't anyone else skiing except the real locals. It was kind of like having my own training facility, like I was Bode Miller on a private mountain. All I had to do was ask the mountain manager where I could set up the course, and he'd point me toward whatever trail he wanted me to use. (I paid them back a couple of times when George Hurt, the general manager at Hidden Valley, found me in the cafeteria or out on the slopes and asked me to fill in for his sick lift operators by stuffing butts on the Poma lift. It didn't matter that I was too young to be working there; all I had to do was sit in the shack, slide the platter between people's legs, and make sure they didn't trip the safety gate.)

Once I got out of high school our race team started to dissolve. So, after my senior year I started working at the ski area full time; I was the assistant foreman on the upper lift, which was something of a privilege for a youngster like me. The following year, they never got the upper mountain open. We kept telling our bosses, "Hey, we need to get up there and set up the snow fences or it'll never happen!" It was the infamous drought year, 1980-'81, and the conditions never filled in up high. So I was stuck on the lower lift with a lot of weary skiers wishing for better snow. I kind of read the writing on the wall that they were running the ski area into the ground. It was time to head for higher ground.

***

The first job I ever had, of any kind, entailed working the register at a video arcade in Estes. I made $1.65 an hour. That segued into a gig at the Go-Kart track, which proved key down the road. I wrenched on karts and learned the basics of heavy machinery, but at the same time, I made friends with whom I stayed in touch long after we left the track.

After my epiphany about Hidden Valley's doomed future, I started wondering where I might go next, and what I might do. Some of the guys I'd worked with at the Go-Kart track were working at Copper Mountain, and they always told me how great the place was.

Itching for a bigger mountain and a break from my hometown, I decided I might as well see if they were right. So at age 20, I packed up all my gear and moved to Copper.

Knowing some of the old Go-Kart guys was a godsend because I had a couch to live on for the first month while I tried to find a job and a place to live. Back then there was no employee housing to speak of, so you were in the rental pool like everyone else. It was a struggle.

Copper was a major resort compared with Hidden Valley. Its covered bubble chair was a huge draw in Colorado. I was thrust into a whole new world of ski bumming. Much of the resort was still under construction, but a lot of the soul that remains today was already in place. Mike and Miguel's was a cool Mexican place that always hosted a hopping happy hour at the end of the day. They had a nacho bar, so employees, myself included, flocked like ants to candy; it was packed every day. If I wasn't there, I was at Farley's or Captain Pepperoni's.

Copper was a great place to work back then. This was primarily because Chuck Lewis, who built the ski area, was a diehard skier himself. Whenever he saw any administrative workers in the office, he'd say to them, "Have you skied today?" If they said no, he'd say, "Well, put on your gear, get out there, and go see what's going on. Your paperwork can wait. Find out how the guests are being treated." All the senior management skied every day of the winter.

It's no surprise that the mountain ran so smoothly back then. They'd make their money and say, What can we do with this? Let's add to the snowmaking, let's upgrade this or that, because it's going to be important.

The first year I worked at Copper was a very dry year. I was a snowmaker, and I remember dragging hoses through the woods to blow snow on trails that didn't have snowmaking. I made snow until February of that year, at which point they finally said, "Well, if it doesn't snow anymore, we're done making snow. We can't afford to keep doing this. When it melts, we're closed."

The company tried to stay open as long as they could back then, to compete with Arapahoe Basin and Loveland. They'd make it into May and a couple of times I think they made it into June. There was very limited skiing, but they did what they could to stay open.

Since it was a resort instead of a town, everybody knew everybody. We were all good friends and we all partied together. If you're seen out partying now, it's like you're a bad person. Back then, if you weren't partying, there was something wrong with you.

That's kind of how life in all of Summit County has changed. Back in the day, Copper was where people from Breckenridge would go to party, because we'd have three or four live bands in the resort every night. You could walk from one show to the next. Now, you're lucky to have even one place that might have a band or, more likely, a solo guitarist.

I know it sounds wistful, but I liked the camaraderie between all the employees back then. Now it's so big I have a hard time getting to know everybody in my own department. I worked 12-hour shifts for much of my 20s, mostly making snow, which didn't leave much time for skiing. In fact, if it weren't for my decision to quit smoking followed by a brutal injury I suffered when I was 40, I might never have started my streak at all.

On the day of my injury, January 6, 2001, I was skiing Patrol Chute at Copper early in the morning. The sky was clear and bluer than the ocean, but as I stood on top of the run, I got this weird feeling in my gut, like something bad was about to happen. Something life-changing.

I looked down the chute and thought to myself, everything looks fine from here. If you always back away in life, you'll never go anywhere. But I should have listened to my gut that day.

I jumped into the chute and skied it well, but at the bottom of the run, a snowboard carve had frozen overnight and had yet to thaw. I essentially hit a concrete curb dead-on with my ski tip. It stopped my leg and snapped it right at the boot top, fracturing my tibia and fibula in an instant. As I tumbled, I heard the crunch of my bones and my body. There was no question my lower leg was destroyed.

A ski instructor and his ski-school kids stopped when they saw me; the guy told his kids to wait there while he went to call it in. I had a cell phone at the time, so I called patrol headquarters. "Hey guys, it's Rainer, I'm at the bottom of Patrol Chute, and I've broken my leg for sure," I told them. "Will you send someone to help me? And could you let my boss, Bruce Hodson, know that I'm not going to be at work tonight?"

They wrapped me up and loaded me into a toboggan then skied me down to the medical center. Later that day, my doctor put in a nail and a couple of screws to secure the fracture. I couldn't ski for three months. Instead, I'd turn up my stereo and hobble out my door on crutches, then do 100 laps up and down the hallway.

I sat on the couch watching all these powder days go by, stuck in my one-bedroom condo because I couldn't drive. My only true friends were the remote control and Andy Held, who would stop by almost daily to play cribbage. As the days dragged on and the flakes floated down outside my window, one thought stuck in my mind.

Someday I'm going to make up for this.

III

The energy in a ski town after a big powder day is unlike anything in the world. You can feel it on the street, in the bars, in the air. Everyone who skied that day walks around with a permanent grin, floating on some kind of magic cloud. I feel more alive after a powder day than I do almost anytime else.

It was after a day like that when my streak first took root in my head. In February 2003, I went up to Jackson Hole, Wyoming, to snowmobile in Yellowstone National Park and visit a couple of resorts for some inbounds powder turns. An old friend named Chad Warnell, who works as a snowmobile mechanic at Copper, joined me, as did a 25-year-old Australian girl I'd met in Sydney some years before. Her name was Jess Smith and, as she says, she tends to party "like it was just invented."

We drove up to Cowboy Village Resort in Jackson then snowmobiled around Togwotee Mountain Lodge, which abuts some of the best terrain in the West. This was back before the National Park Service began heavily regulating snowmobile traffic in Yellowstone; we got in and out without much trouble or hassle, and spent the night at "Old Faithful" — a small cabin that cost $70.

After our motorized adventures, we spent a couple of days skiing at Jackson Hole then Grand Targhee, a more laid-back powder mecca on the west side of the Tetons. The Jackson day ended, like all Jackson powder days do for me, at the Mangy Moose.

If you've never been to the Mangy Moose, it is like walking

into a museum where cowboys and skiers share the same DNA. The Moose opened in 1967, shortly after the ski resort opened. Inside, a giant stuffed moose hangs on the wall and eclectic wooden finishes gives the bar a feeling of coziness that has characterized Western ski towns for decades.

I had always kept track of how much vertical I skied, so my mind was already thinking in terms of statistics when I stumbled past a plaque on the wall that night at the Moose. The plaque honored a group of people who had skied 6 million vertical feet in a season. The list included only a handful of names. *Huh,* I thought, *a Six Million Club. I think I can do that.*

Almost simultaneously, and pretty much instinctively, it became my goal for the following season. I figured if I skied every day of the winter, essentially averaging 33,000 vertical feet a day for six months, I'd hit it by April or May.

The year before, at the end of the spring of 2002, I had wrapped my season only 130,000 feet short of 4 million. So when I set off on a motorcycle trip to Alaska that summer, I stopped at Mt. Hood for a week and skied 30,000 feet a day to pass the four-million mark. I remembered the feeling of satisfaction — elation, really — that hitting 4 million feet brought me. I felt like I'd achieved something worthwhile. It motivated me to stay true to my goal of increasing the number to 6 million feet the next year.

I got home from Alaska in September 2003 and ended up riding my motorcycle for another 5,000 miles around Colorado since the weather was so good. But once it started getting cold, I put the bike away and focused on the snow.

Copper opened on November 1, 2003, but employees weren't supposed to go skiing that day because it was such a madhouse on the lone open run — what we affectionately call "the white ribbon of death." But I went skiing anyway. I figured if I was going to make a run at this 6 Million Club, I needed to start immediately and I needed to start logging vert.

I got in trouble right off the bat. Jim Spenst, the mountain manager and director of operations at Copper, was standing in the lift maze greeting guests, and he saw me. I'd known Jim for decades since he used to be in charge of lift operations and maintenance. He'd always liked the quality of work I did, but, alas, rules are rules.

"Are you working now?" he asked.

"No," I said, knowing that made my presence on the slopes a violation of policy. To soften the infraction, I explained that I had just skied down the open run when I spotted a fallen tree that had broken in half and was lying across the trail. It was a legitimate hazard, so I stopped and picked up the top half of the tree and placed it behind the closure rope. It kept us from having a liability, and due to the opening-day crowds and finite terrain, ski patrol wasn't skiing, the trail crew wasn't skiing, there was actually nobody patrolling the slopes unless someone called in an injury. So I felt like I helped out the overall cause … even if it made my own plight more attainable.

Jim didn't entirely buy my excuse, but he had more important issues to manage that day. "OK, Rainer, whatever," he said, and sent me on my way with a little growl. I appreciated his understanding.

I started grooming a few days later and fell into my winter routine, which would carry me through the next eight years. It went like this: wake up, ski as much as time or the conditions allowed, hustle home for lunch, head to work, get some sleep, repeat.

I kept plugging away at my goal. The winter went pretty well, all things considered — no significant injuries, ample if not epic snow — but it had its share of hurdles too. We endured some rotten weather days and certain lifts didn't open sometimes due to wind and mechanical problems. But since I wasn't aiming for a world record at the time, I wasn't too concerned. I just put my head down and kept skiing.

***

By scheduling my life around skiing as much as I could, day in and day out, I ended up hitting 6 million feet right about when I thought I would. I crossed the magic number on Cinco de Mayo 2004 — five days later than the six-month window I'd envisioned, but I didn't care. With the milestone in the bag, my goal suddenly evolved into something more tied to a consecutive-days streak. I hadn't missed a day since November 1, so, I thought, there's still plenty of ski season left, why not see where this goes?

Copper and Loveland — two of my go-to resorts — had already closed, but I had plenty of time to maintain the streak at Arapahoe Basin, which was still trying to stay open as late as possible in those days. (Some years they even made it to the Fourth of July.)

On the day I passed 7 million feet, I was riding up the Pallavicini lift at A-Basin — a classic old double chair that accesses 1,300 feet of steeps — and I thought, I don't know of a 7 Million Club. I could be sitting on a record here. Since I hadn't told Stan Miller that I was coming back to work that summer as a heavy equipment operator, I was essentially a free agent. I had enough money in the bank that I didn't really need to work right away. So I figured I might as well see if I could keep going.

Knowing that Colorado's ski season would soon be over and that I would have to make it to Mt. Hood if I wanted to give it a second life, I decided to spend the summer in Oregon.

In order not to miss a day, I had to be around snow for some part of every 24-hour period, including travel days. This is not as easy as it sounds. But it is realistic if you want it badly enough.

A-Basin closed on June 17, 2004, so when I went to ski that day, I had my bike already packed, with skis on it. At the end of the day, I rode up to Hayden, near Steamboat Springs, and stayed at a friend's house. I called another friend in the Park City, Utah, area to ask about staying with him the next night. He agreed, so I rode toward Utah the next morning. On my way, I stopped at Wolf Creek Pass, Utah, and looked around for a while. I finally found a patch of snow a mile off the road that was maybe seven vertical feet. I skied back and forth on that patch of snow, going down one side then up the other side, for two hours straight. I figure I skied about two miles on that patch of snow. Then I continued on to Park City.

My friend was still working when I arrived, so instead of sitting in the bar for two hours waiting for him to get off work, I headed up Guardsman Pass and found a patch of snow to ski the next morning.

After bidding my buddy adieu in Park City, I rode up to

Guardsman, skinned up the quarter-mile-long drift of snow that I scouted the prior evening, skied down it, then I climbed up a switchback and did about seven turns on that, and called it skiing. I took a picture of the tracks for proof.

From Utah, I needed one more stopover before I reached Mt. Hood. I called my old buddy Smoothy, or Brian Amundsen, if we're using real names. He lived up at Tamarack, a fledgling ski resort in Idaho. None of the lifts had been built, but they'd cut a road to the top of the mountain and he said there was a patch of skiable snow near the top. I arrived that afternoon and crashed with him in the campground where he was living, along with the rest of the men and women who were building the ski area.

The next morning, he gave me a ride up Tamarack on the service road, showed me the trails they were cutting, where they were excavating for the ski lifts, and where the lodges and ski-patrol shack were going to go. Then he dropped me off and I skied down a ramshackle run to feed my streak its daily dose of turns.

I made it most of the way to Timberline that afternoon before pitching my tent on a mountain pass near Prineville. The next day, I arrived a bit late to Timberline so I took one for the streak and bought a lift ticket. After skiing, I went down to the base area and met up with some friends who were groomers there. I also met Steve Kruse, who is still the GM of mountain operations, and when I told him what I was up to, he offered to help me out with a few lift tickets.

As it happened, I had taught some of Timberline's groomers how to drive a snowcat many years earlier. So when they introduced me to their boss, Jeff Flood, I had instant credibility. Flood-o (that's what everyone called Jeff) was at his wit's end with the workload he and his team had been dealing with. "You know what," he said, "it's really hot right now, we're super busy, and we're working till 4 in the morning to get the grooming done, which is unacceptable for the racers, because they're on the hill at 6 and the snow has no setup time."

He looked at me. "We have enough cats, so if you could just groom this one area for us, then whenever you're done you can leave and we'll pay you a wage and give you a ski pass." All at once, the next chapter of my ski streak was put in motion.

I skied every day, got off early enough that I could have a decent dinner then go back to my campsite and sleep, then got up early and went skiing again. That summer was the easiest of them all because I was just a part-time guy and didn't have to work late. When my job melted away, they let me keep my pass for the rest of the season because I'd showed everyone that I was serious about my streak, and they wanted to support me.

As I neared the end of the summer, I began to wonder, Now what? I could keep hiking for turns every day because the snow was still there, but I wouldn't get the vertical I was aiming for. On the other hand, I'd always wanted to ski in South America, and I had about four grand in the bank. I scoped out Chilean and Argentine ski areas as well as I could on the Internet and started figuring out where I could get the best vertical.

Armed with that info and that info alone, I bought a ticket to Santiago, Chile. The next step was figuring out how I would bridge the gap between hemispheres without missing a day on skis. A longtime friend of mine, "T-Bar Tommy" Larkin, would later refer to this process as "a military move." But really all it took was the same stubborn persistence that defined the rest of my streak.

I booked my flight for the Wednesday after Labor Day. I did that because we closed on Labor Day, meaning I'd still have lift access that day, then everyone who was still around the ski area participated in trash pickup day on Tuesday, which, again, guaranteed mechanized access to the snow: They drive a snowcat up and drop everybody off, and then everyone walks down and picks up all the garbage from the ski and snowboard camps and sets the bags on the lava next to the snow. I'd talked to Bill Brett, the assistant mountain manager, about taking my skis along. Since they knew about my streak, they were fine with it. So I got a run in, and I picked up a full bag of trash on my way down. It was probably a three-hour run for 1,500 vertical feet.

I broke down my camp and packed my bags after my run. That night, shortly after midnight, my buddy Jake Engle, whom I trained at Copper and who helped get me the job at Timberline, took me and his girlfriend up in a cat then drove back down. We didn't ask for permission, we just did it. I didn't know if I was going to get asked back to work the next summer, so I wasn't thinking about repercussions.

It was a full-moon night, but by the time the moon popped over the ridge, we were already back to the car. I didn't mind the dark skiing; the only thing that mattered was I had skied that day, which essentially gave me a 46-hour buffer before I had to ski again to keep the streak alive.

After Jake and his girlfriend went home, I slept in Charlie's Mountain View, the bar at the base of the resort. At sunrise I drove down to Portland and boarded my flight to Santiago.

***

It was a dry year for the Andes, so by the time I got to South America a bunch of ski areas had already closed or were soon to close. Valle Nevado was one of the few resorts that had had a good season snow-wise -- and its high-speed Andes Express chairlift really allows you to rack up vertical -- so I headed there first, 35 miles outside the city.

It happened that the resort's general manager, Jimmy Ackerson — who once followed winter for 26 consecutive seasons, 13 in each hemisphere — knew Arnie Wilson, the British journalist who skied 365 days in a row and set a Guinness World Record (I was unaware of Wilson's streak at the time). So when I told Jimmy what I was up to, he was eager to help. I got to know some locals and a number of the ski-area employees, which would come in handy in future years. Jimmy upgraded my hotel room at no charge, and I basically skied my brains out until they closed the Andes Express.

From Valle Nevado, I caught a ride to Nevados de Chillan, an active volcano that is also a fine ski area, and skied there until they closed. The vice president even gave me a bonus day when he let me ride the lifts on their employee ski day. The day after their lifts closed once and for all, I hiked up the volcano and skied 800 vertical feet of melting snow to record my run for the day. Then I caught a bus down to Pucon, where some locals told me I'd find decent snow.

The ski area had already closed, but Pucon, like Chillan, is an active volcano that holds snow much later than the lifts run. After a few days of hiking for turns there, I rented a car and barely made it over an unplowed mountain pass to Corralco, a small ski area on the Lonquimay volcano within the Malalcahuello-Nalcas National Reserve.

The ski area was only open on weekends, so I skied the first four days by hiking and ascending with climbing skins attached to the bottom of my skis, then I skied through the weekend while they were open. On my last morning I hiked up to the top of the Poma lift, skied a quick run, jumped in the car, and drove to Victoria where I'd arranged to have the rental company pick it up. They met me at the bus station, and I bought a ticket to Santiago on what they called the "Express Bus." Yeah, right. It turned out the Express Bus stopped to pick up anybody who was hitchhiking on the side of the road.

I was already cutting it close to make my flight, so when I saw a sign that said "Santiago: 100 km," I started to get nervous. For some reason, though, when you get that close to the city, people are riding the train more than the bus, so you're not stopping to pick up as many hitchhikers. I made my flight with an hour to spare.

I landed in Denver midmorning the next day and arranged with a shuttle company to get dropped off at Loveland Ski Area, on the Continental Divide. It was early October and Loveland had just opened for the season. I stashed my luggage in someone's office and skied the rest of the day. Then my friend Kelly Heil picked me up and brought me home to Copper.

Once I got back from Chile, I figured, now I *really* don't have an excuse to quit. I'd made it through all the logistical hurdles down there, which was tough: I didn't know any Spanish, I didn't know where any of the ski areas were, I didn't know anyone in South America, I even got a bunch of flat tires on my rental car.

Back home in Colorado, with my own transportation and local routine, I finally felt like I could complete a year of daily skiing. Coincidentally, since I had begun on November 1, 2003, my final day of the year fell on Halloween. And perhaps to help me celebrate, Ullr, the Norse God of Snow, saw fit to pummel us with powder that day.

Copper's bosses were letting me ski with the race camps that October because they knew what I was trying to do. I skied for 7 hours and 49 minutes on Halloween, mostly because the snow was awesome and I had nothing better to do. When I called it a day, I threw my skis over my shoulder and started walking through the base area to my condo. The Denver TV station Fox31 was there to do a story on the early season snowstorm, and when they saw me with my big icicle mustache, their reporter asked if they could do an interview. She was an attractive dark-haired woman in high heels. I told her I'd just completed a year of daily skiing and that it might be a world record, but I wasn't really sure of it. We talked for a while then parted ways. I couldn't wait to see the interview on the news that night — a cool reward for completing a year.

Well, as the Fox31 crew was driving back to Denver, some lady drove off Interstate 70 and got winched back up just west of the Eisenhower Tunnel. They stopped and reported on what happened, then decided to nix my interview in favor of the stupid accident. I couldn't believe it. Something that happens every day made the news instead of ... well, come to think of it, something else that happens every day. Only, my version is more fun than crashing in a ravine.

IV

After I passed a year of skiing, more people noticed what I was doing. The one-year mark legitimized it in a sense. I wasn't just *trying* to ski for a year. I had.

People who didn't ski couldn't grasp it as well as those who skied. If you skied, you could sit down and think about skiing every day for an entire year. You could understand what it might take. Kind of.

I became a small-time celebrity at Copper. Every big ski resort in the West sees its share of turnover, but there are a lot of us who have worked at Copper for 25 or 30 years. I know all of them and they all know me. People congratulated me on my feat. I appreciated their comments but also made it clear I had no intention of stopping.

I've always been stubborn when it comes to skiing. I don't like to give it up unless I absolutely have to. When I was in my early teens, I broke my leg and had to walk around in a cast that went from my toe to my hip. But it didn't stop me from skiing; I put a trash bag over my cast and skied down the Poma on one ski. Eventually, my mom let me ride and ski the lower T-bar and then the upper T. I got nicknamed "The Man From GLAD," not only due to the bag on my leg, but because I was really glad to be skiing instead of moping around the house.

In the case of my streak, skiing had become the driving force in my life. I planned every detail with skiing in mind. It had always showed me the best times of my life, and now it was giving me purpose. A kind of purpose people in their 40s crave.

Skiing did something similar for me in 1995 when it helped me quit smoking — which, you could say, paved the way for my streak a decade later.

I had gone down to work for a friend at the Kowhai Lodge at Lake Coleridge on the South Island of New Zealand during the northern hemisphere's summer.

At the time, I was smoking two packs of cigarettes a day. That was actually less than I normally smoked, but they cost so much in New Zealand that I couldn't afford more than two packs a day, even buying them by the carton. I'd been a smoker for most of my life; I smoked my first cigarette when I was five or six years old. My dad smoked, so I'd steal them out of his pack, or I'd pick up an old butt on the sidewalk or in the gutter. It's gross to think about that now.

The worst thing about my smoking is that I almost never skied when I smoked. I partied a lot back then and maybe skied a couple of days a week. When I did ski, it wasn't for more than five or six runs.

I was staying in a town called Omarama during the 1995 Gliding World Championships for fixed-wing aircraft, and had been thinking about quitting smoking for years. My Kiwi friend Ric Georgeson kept poking me, saying, "Damn, Rainer, you stink all the time, you just smell like cigarettes." So that was bugging me, and I finally came to grips with reality: it's a habit that doesn't give you a buzz and is very expensive. I thought if I can just quit these stupid things, I'll save tons of money and travel more and have a better life overall.

To be honest, as much as I was addicted to nicotine, I was also addicted to the social side of smoking. If you think about the Marlboro Man or John Wayne or any of the tough guys smoking cigarettes — that *look* — it's easy to think they're tough because they're smoking a cigarette. My mental, visual fear of not having a cigarette hanging out of my mouth at all times was part of my addiction.

I was sitting at a bar on New Year's Eve in Omarama during

the gliding worlds. My friend Ric's father — we called him the Captain — is a big deal in the gliding world, and Ric was there cleaning toilets as an event volunteer. I was helping Ric and sharing a tent at night. After work, I'd gone to a bar and had cocktails and was smoking, and the bartender said, "You look really depressed, what the hell's going on?" My grandmother had passed away not too long ago, but the thought of quitting smoking monopolized my mind.

"I'm quitting smoking tonight," I told her — and she could see I meant it.

"Wow," she said. "Here, have another drink."

About two months after I quit, while I was still in New Zealand, I got really upset about something and rolled up three cigarettes. The tobacco was called Port Royal. It had been soaked in rum and sat on our bookshelf for two months. Talk about stale, repulsive tobacco. I took down all three cigarettes in a row, and it was so horrible that I never picked up another one after that. I have puffed on cigars for kids' birthdays and other occasions, but after two or three tokes off a cigar, I'm about green and gagging.

It was cool that Ric was around to see me quit cigarettes. He was a big part of the reason why I did — a friend who cared enough to say something. There's actually a funny story behind how we met.

In 1990, I was part of an American team hired to upgrade some ski facilities at Mt. Hutt, which is also on the South Island. I spent a few months making snow and training people to make snow. It was a month before the World Cup races were scheduled to take place at Mt. Hutt, and the technical delegate ("TD") from the ski federation showed up and approved the work we'd done, confirming the races for the following month. (Those races basically put New Zealand on the world map for alpine skiing.)

On one of my rare days off, I went to the Blue Pub to drink for the night. The area around Mt. Hutt was really desolate back then: one gas station, a few restaurants, only a handful of residents. The Blue Pub was in Methven, a town about 40 minutes from Mt. Hutt. I'd met a few of the local girls who were younger than I, and as luck would have it, seven of them wanted to go out partying. They approached me and one of them said, "Will you be our chaperone tonight? No one's going to mess with you because you're a big guy."

"Sure," I said. "Let's go out and rip it up!"

We hit all the bars downtown before deciding to head to a new disco bar that had just opened. It was fancy schmancy compared with all the other bars, which were more like farmhand or ski-bum bars. (People around Mt. Hutt were either sheep herders or ski bums.)

The fancy place was about a half-mile out of town. We were partying, I was dancing with two girls at a time, and Ric — the only other man in the place besides the bartender and disco guy — was sitting at the bar wondering what on earth he was watching.

"How'd you score all these girls?" he asked me.

Understand, Ric is a woman's man. He picks up chicks like a magnet picks up paperclips. Looking back on that night, I'm sure I made quite the first impression, but there was no pretension. We introduced ourselves, I told him how I came to party with seven younger girls, and we learned each of us was into skiing. Then it started absolutely pouring — what I call upside-down rain: you get soaked from below because it's bouncing up off the pavement so hard.

"Hey," I said to Ric, "any chance you could give us all a ride home?"

"No problem," he said.

Ric had a car called a Lada, a Russian four-wheel-drive vehicle that's similar to a Subaru but shorter. So the seven girls and I all piled into this little thing and Ric dropped everyone off at their homes. I was the last stop and he ended up crashing at my place. We were renting a house called the U.S. Embassy because five Americans lived there (we also had a Canadian roommate, but he didn't mind the name). We were working different shifts and catching rides up the hour-long, treacherous road to the ski area. All the locals knew our house: We hung an American flag from the lightning rod on the roof and spray painted a board that said "U.S. Embassy" on the hedge in front of the entry. In the middle of the winter we threw a Fourth of July party with seven kegs, which were almost empty by the time I got off work. Only three local guys were still at the party, but apparently it was a hoot. We shot off fireworks at 1 a.m. to celebrate America's independence.

Ric is a full-blooded Kiwi and is well known in that area. I went back and stayed with him in '95 then saw him again when I returned in 2001. I was down there to work, but I also took my mom as a one-time gift to thank her for everything she put up with while I was growing up … which was a lot.

After my work was finished, we rented an RV and toured around for a while, saw some other ski areas. Every road in New Zealand is utterly gorgeous to drive.

After three months Mom headed back to the U.S. and I stayed. That's about when 9/11 happened. It was weird watching the aftermath of those attacks from afar. What they were showing in the rest of the world was not what they were showing in the U.S. In the U.S., everyone was talking about how anthrax was going to spread and how there would be more attacks, so I actually started to apply for residency in New Zealand. I was in one of the safest places in the world, the final frontier, so why would I leave? I would've had to give up everything I owned, but at the time it seemed like a logical option.

After talking to people back home, however, they made me realize that it wasn't as bad as it seemed from afar. I didn't need to move to New Zealand.

***

I started skiing a lot more after I quit cigarettes. Not just more often, but for longer. I think it was because I felt healthier, and one of the reasons I felt healthier was because I was skiing more. I started to appreciate again the purity of linking turns down the mountain. I felt like I was young and creative and hungry again.

Still, at no point did I ever think I would someday ski more than anyone else ever had. Shit, I didn't even realize I broke the world record the day I broke it. I would've had to know a record for consecutive ski days existed.

That day, No. 366, happened to be Halloween, the final day of my first year, which fell in a leap year. The fact that it completed a full year was far more significant at the time. Only later did I find out that Arnie Wilson and Lucy Dicker had skied 365 straight days in 1994, earning a place in the Guinness Book of World Records.

Arnie was the ski correspondent for the Financial Times in England. He and I had a bit of a troubled relationship early on, but we later made up and had a few really nice conversations, and have been on good terms ever since.

Shortly after I passed a year, Arnie got in touch with me and told me about his streak. I don't remember if it was by phone or e-mail, but as time went on, he sent me a few e-mails about random funny stuff, and I didn't always have time to read them. I said something in an interview with Outside Magazine leading up to my 1,000th day — something about Arnie thinking we had a relationship because of our shared pursuits, but that I felt like he was just some guy in England.

Well, he saw the article and one of his colleagues at Ski and Board Magazine sent me a pretty irate note. Arnie was very offended himself. The Outside quote got misconstrued, but I never meant to hurt him. Nor was I ever trying to beat his streak. In fact, the more I learned about his streak, the more respect I had for him and Lucy and what they achieved, even if they went about it differently than I did.

Arnie had been thinking about skiing every day of a calendar year since 1990, when Vogue Magazine asked him to write a story about how one might ski every month of the year. Two years later, he and Lucy — a pretty French woman from Provence — met on a press trip to the French Alps (she sold ski vacations from London), and in 1994 they set off to ski every day for a year, with Arnie writing weekly dispatches for the Financial Times.

They were on the move for almost the entire year. Averaging about two resorts every three days, they ended up skiing at 237 different areas in 13 countries and on five continents. Like me, they were obsessed with statistics, but unlike me, they measured their ski days more by horizontal mileage than vertical descent. They aimed for 10 miles a day, as quantified by a little device mounted on the back of their boots. (I tracked my numbers first by hand and then with a Suunto watch. More on that later.)

Thanks to Arnie's press contacts (he's well known in London, having worked for seven national newspapers and seven television stations), they got most of their lift tickets for free, and often their accommodations too. They had two airline sponsors, a rental-car sponsor — even Ski the Summit, which was based in Summit County, Colorado, where I live, sponsored them to gain exposure.

Arnie and Lucy started in Jackson Hole and gradually made their way to New York. They mostly drove from ski area to ski area, linking big and small, famous and unknown resorts alike through America's heartland. Of course they spent plenty of time in the West, including a lengthy stay in Colorado, but they also skied in Kentucky, Indiana, Alabama, and Illinois. They, like me, flew down to South America during the southern hemisphere winter, and they often made predawn runs to cover their travel days. Their closest call came in Chile, where one day they got so gooned by their rental car that they didn't get to ski until 11 p.m. They shuttled each other up and down a volcano in the pouring rain.

Whereas I took a job in Oregon to be near summer snow, they spent nine weeks in South America, then another nine weeks in Australia and New Zealand. They also skied in the Himalayas and around Europe.

Their sponsors dramatically lowered the cost of their trip but also created a list of people they felt beholden to. Arnie says they often got in arguments over that. He was tempted to abandon the trip multiple times and would tell Lucy, "You can carry on and damn well ski for the sponsors. I'm going home." Some days they didn't even ski the same mountain.

But they always stuck it out. His biggest adventure leading up to that trip was riding around the world on a molasses tanker when he was 19. Shortly after they started dating, Lucy told him she had always wanted a big adventure in her life. Their round-the-world ski trip provided that.

On the last day of their streak, ironically enough, they skied Breckenridge, Keystone, and Copper. A PR entourage led them around Breckenridge, where they were crowned "king and queen of skiing." Thirty ski patrollers guided them down the hill at Copper.

And a guitar player serenaded them at the base of Keystone's gondola, where they were served tea and scones. Someone even strung a pseudo finish line across the bottom of their last run to mark the occasion. Their total tally was 4.1 million vertical feet and 3,678 miles. They even kept track of how many times they fell: 128 for Lucy, 127 for Arnie.

Lucy wanted to keep skiing at the end of their streak, but Arnie had to get back to work and earn some money. They kept dating, but a few months after their streak wrapped, another adventure ended tragically.

On April 6, 1995, Arnie and Lucy were among a group of nine skiers, including a guide, exploring the endless couloirs around La Grave, France. They had skied mostly powder that day when the guide peered into a lesser-known tube of snow and asked the group if they wanted to ski it. Lucy said no; she didn't think she was good enough. Another client reassured her: "Come on, Lucy. If I can ski it, you can."

Although the guide was heavily criticized later for taking the group down the couloir, Lucy agreed to ski it. Arnie was among the first people down, and when he looked back up, he saw a horrifying sight. Somehow Lucy and Arnie's best friend, Peter Hardy, had collided and were now sliding down the icy chute at rapidly escalating speeds. Arnie could tell that Lucy was unconscious. As she careened past him like a rag doll, he lunged for her limp body and held on, creating a tandem mass of flailing limbs and ski gear. They slid for a couple hundred feet then launched off a mound of snow, separating in the air. When everyone came to a rest, Lucy was bleeding heavily. Peter was still conscious but also badly injured. The friction during the fall was so hot that it burned a hole in Arnie's ski suit and left a wide abrasion on his skin.

Rescue helicopters quickly descended on the group and medics began pumping Lucy's chest to keep her alive. They took Lucy and Peter to separate hospitals. Lucy died on the way to Grenoble. Arnie was left on the mountain to ski down to La Grave.

The sad story had a happy ending. Five years after that accident, in 2000, Arnie married a Swedish woman at the top of

Jackson Hole Mountain Resort. Peter Hardy, by then fully recovered from his injuries, served as his best man. Arnie and Lucy still hold the Guinness World Record for most distance skied in a year.

***

All things considered, my second year was smoother than my first. My girlfriend at the time, Ginger Gamage, contacted Guinness about recognizing my streak, and in March we found out that they'd created a category for me: most vertical feet skied in consecutive days on telemark gear. I guess they wanted to distinguish between freeheel and fixed-heel skiing, even if it's all just sliding down mountains on planks when you think about it.

Probably the most eerie day of my entire streak happened two months later, on Friday, May 20. I was skiing at A-Basin, lapping the Pali chair all morning. I had also been there the day before and skied through the afternoon. The snow was getting really hollow toward the end of the day. I was punching through moguls into the lower layers of the snowpack. It was bizarre, but I didn't think much of it.

On my way up Highway 6 Friday morning, I noticed an avalanche in a nearby backcountry stash called the Beavers that hadn't been there when I went home the prior day. It was hardly alarming, but I basically stuck to groomers that morning. Around 10:30 a.m., I had to use the bathroom and went into the lodge. When I came out and got on Pali again, I saw all kinds of resort employees racing uphill on snowmobiles toward the base of the steep Pali face. Not even a minute into my lift ride, I saw that the entire First Alley had ripped out. When I got to the top, a ski patroller told me the face was closed due to the avalanche.

Everyone around the patroller was offering to go get probe poles from their cars and help with the search for victims, but they asked us to just keep skiing. A couple of hours later, it became obvious someone had been killed. They brought a victim down in a toboggan, and people were walking away from him shaking their heads. A Flight for Life helicopter landed. The Summit County Sheriff's Office showed up, then the county coroner.

The victim was a 53-year-old Boulder man named David Conway. He hadn't done anything wrong, just skied the First Alley on a beautiful May day. The snow hadn't refrozen overnight, however, and it was heavy and wet and ripe to slide. No one witnessed the avalanche, which amazes me, but it caught Conway and basically cleaned out an 800-vertical foot tree run to the ground, leaving a huge debris pile at the bottom.

It was freaky to see that happen at a ski area. I've always understood that skiing is dangerous, and even when we control the snow it's still a natural environment with unpredictable risks. The only two avalanches I've ever been caught in happened at Hidden Valley when I was 16, in what we called First Bowl: I rolled out of one as it thundered into a stand of trees, and got buried up to my waist by another. At A-Basin, I kept saying that my guardian angels were looking after me. It could have been anyone dropping into the First Alley that day. Since then I have tele'd some sloughs of loose powder and learned that as long as you keep the same speed — fast — and don't make any mistakes, it's really fun. But a wet slab avalanche like the one that killed Conway is a different ballgame entirely. Once it has you in its grips, you have no control over what happens.

My season continued up to the Pacific Northwest after A-Basin closed. I set up my camp in the woods near Timberline on June 14, just in time to hop on the chairlift and take a few runs before the mountain closed. Well, no one got the message that my chair was the last chair that day, so the lifties stopped the lift while I was still on it. It was cloudy enough that neither the top, midway, nor bottom terminal workers could see me. Luckily, they ran the lift backward for a minute, and when I arrived at the midway terminal, I jumped off, thankful I would not be spending the night on the chair.

That summer was a rainy one, not only to be camping but also to be skiing. The good part was the rain kept the crowds down. The bad part was it drenched you. I would wear my motorcycle rain gear and a full-face helmet, and I bought some rubber dishwashing gloves that kept my hands dry. I was always kind of hesitant to go skiing in the rain, but once I was out there, as long as I stayed dry it didn't bother me at all.

I didn't get to see much family during my streak, but in early August, my Aunt Luise's 70th birthday party attracted a large number of relatives to Whidbey Island, Washington, about five hours north of Timberline. I didn't want to miss it, but I also didn't want to miss a day of skiing. So I got a little creative.

I had always worried about a flight getting canceled in a warm city, like when I connected through Atlanta on my way to Chile. How would I ski? In case that ever happened, I came up with an idea that would be my emergency plan: skiing on ice.

I tried it at my Uncle Adolf's house once. On a day when the weather on Mt. Hood was about the worst I'd seen, I knew the lifts were going to be closed so I bought a bunch of bags of ice, mowed the lawn really short, then dumped out the ice and raked it so I could ski. And it worked! Far out!

The slope was maybe three feet wide. I laid the ice into a long "S" and pretty much just slid down until I stopped on the grass. Then I'd run back up and do it again. The ice lasted a while that day because it was rainy and cold; I think I did 30 runs.

That day also happened to be when one of my Uncle Adolf's long-lost Army buddies was visiting. He'd found Uncle Adolf on the Internet after not seeing each other for 50 years, and made plans to reunite in Oregon. Their stories were a bonus for me after my ice test worked out.

Back in the '50s, Uncle Adolf and his buddy, Helmut Burns, fabricated a raft out of four 55-gallon drums and some arctic pine trees, pitched a tent on top, and floated down the Yukon River to Alakanuk, Alaska. One afternoon they spotted a cabin along the river's edge and stopped in to say hi. Since no one was there, they tied up the raft and planned to spend the night. The owner of the cabin arrived a bit later, but he didn't mind the company. Uncle Adolf and Helmut shared some of their supplies, and the frontiersman pulled out a jug of whiskey and passed it around. It was the kind of story every worthy adventure includes.

Having successfully tested my ice-skiing method, I put it to use at my Aunt Luise's birthday party. A few days before my trip, I called ahead to a grocery store on Whidbey Island. "I want to reserve 50 bags of ice," I told them. They said they always stocked plenty of ice for fishermen, and that I could just pick it up when I got there. But I couldn't take the chance of them running out. "This is really important," I explained, "so let me just pay for it now." It was easily my most expensive lift ticket.

I rode my motorcycle up to the Whidbey Island ferry, took it across to the island, then borrowed someone's car to pick up the ice. I'd left my skis with my cousin in Portland, since he was driving up in a car. He got there that afternoon, and my circus began.

The party was at my cousin Sarah's house, right on the water. I spread out my 50 bags of ice on the sand, again in an "S" formation to allow me to turn. The slope was about 10 or 15 vertical feet, and I had to do it at low tide so I had enough room to descend. Twenty of my relatives were there for the reunion and party. Luise was my father's sister, but my mom was there too, since she was always close with his family. As I set up my run, everyone was standing around laughing hysterically. Someone even filmed it.

I looked like a beach bum, not a ski bum, in my swim trunks and bare chest. It didn't matter. I strapped on my skis and buckled my boots, then pushed off down the handcrafted ski surface. It was funny as hell. I did 12 runs, finishing five feet below sea level every time. I only stopped skiing because the ice melted.

Since I had been a snowmaker for so many years, I figured that this qualified as snow skiing since it is basically the same as manmade snow — frozen water arranged on the earth for skiing.

"We'll never forget this," my Aunt Luise said.

Neither will I.

The next morning, I caught the first ferry back to the mainland and rode my motorcycle five hours back to Timberline. I got there in time to ski for two hours and 22 minutes that afternoon.

The adventures continued in South America two weeks later, rather inauspiciously at first. After picking up my rental car in Santiago, I got lost. I drove around the city for hours, trying to figure out where I was and how to get up to the mountains. Since it was totally overcast, I couldn't see the mountains to get my bearing and get out of Santiago. By the time I finally made it close to Portillo, it was nearly dark and my only option was climbing up a slope on the side of the road. I skied 160 vertical feet and called it a day.

Since there were no rooms left at Portillo, I spent the night in my rental car. But as beautiful as it was, the full moon was so bright that I never fell asleep.

I skied at Portillo the next two days, with an interlude to track down what they call *seguro de automores* — proof of car insurance, which you need to cross the border and drive in Argentina. I got the little piece of paper in a small hut across some railroad tracks in Los Andes, down the hill from Portillo. Then I set off to meet my brother at Las Leñas in Argentina. I ended up driving down a dirt access road in the dark of night, surrounded by vast, open ranchland. I started to nod off.

Suddenly I awoke to see a herd of black cattle, almost invisible in the midnight blackness, standing in the middle of the road. I screeched to a stop and sat in my car shaking. Soon after, the moon rose above the mountains and I continued on, rolling into Las Leñas at 1 a.m.

Due to a few weeks of bad weather, I spent plenty of time at Las Leñas, the most extreme ski area I've ever skied. They bomb for avalanches through the night there, and when you walk out a gate to ski the 3,000-foot chutes, you have to show the ski patrollers your passport and they strap a Recco band to your helmet, which helps them find you under the snow. Then they write down your name and passport information so that it's easier to identify your corpse, should the need arise.

From Las Leñas, I embarked on a tour of Andean ski areas. Like Caviahue: a tiny place situated in an araucaria forest where you can ski through 300-year-old "monkey puzzle trees" studded with two-inch-long thorns. And Cerro Bayo: a spectacular and surprisingly steep mountain where free-range cattle graze right up to the edge of the snow in spring.

I passed through Bariloche, a more modern resort, and continued on to La Hoya, a small and very snowy ski area near the Patagonian town of Esquel, where Butch Cassidy used to hole up back in the day. To get there, you drive through a military checkpoint where they only take their finger off the machine-gun trigger if they have to check your passport. I think that's why crime is fairly low in that region.

While at La Hoya, I met a ski patroller who was wearing a fly-fishing cap from Durango, Colorado. We got to talking, I told him I was from Colorado and what I was up to. We've kept in touch since then, sharing stories now and again, and he always updates me on the local ski conditions.

Patagonia was as far south as I got. I crossed the border back into Chile, explored two more small ski areas named Antillanca (which is located on an extinct volcano) and Pucon (which was designed by my friend Claudio Diaz). Claudio still had some connections with Pucon's managers, so I scored a few comp tickets there. I had hiked for turns my first year in Pucon, and by this time I'd told a few of the locals what I was up to. That helped me build a rapport in town, particularly among the workers at my hotel. People know each other there; the gossip moves around pretty quickly. They had sent me to an unreal steakhouse. Two huge beef tenderloins, as wide as they were thick, for under $10. Veggies are extra: your baked potato is a buck, your beer is a buck. It was heaven.

I gave the guy at the restaurant a hat, and he said, "Amigo, you are a local here, 10 percent off."

From Pucon I blazed on to Corralco and then Termas de Chillan. Near the end of my stay there, I met two telemark skier girls from Alaska. They were in their 20s, fun-loving people who didn't take life too seriously, which was my outlook too. Turns out they were on the same program I was — wandering around the Andes, skiing, and partying. We got to know each other and figured, why not travel together?

After some discussion, we piled into my rental car and headed for Farellones, a centrally located ski hub about 25 miles outside Santiago. We hit El Colorado, La Parva, and my favorite, Valle Nevado. Since they were on a tight budget and some of the areas had closed for the season, they would skin up the closed ones and have a great time checking things out while I rode lifts and slaughtered vertical. After a few more days they headed back to Alaska, and not much later, Valle Nevado closed for the season.

Once that happened, I started to hitchhike-ski from my rental car at the base of Santa Maria, a cool steep run with cliff belts mixed in. I got lucky a couple of times and scored snowcat rides from where the cars dropped me off, allowing for extra vertical, but mostly I just clicked in and skied back to my car.

The road was situated precisely where winter changed to spring, as the uphill side was snow and the downhill side was bone dry, with lizards and orange tarantulas running around in the dirt. I asked my friend Claudio Diaz why there were so many spiders, and he said it was the year of the babies. They were about two inches around and always a striking sight to see after I had just skied down.

One day I saw a pair of falcons mating in the same spot, just on the other side of a snow bank. Another day I took a break from skiing in the rain and fell asleep to the soothing splatter of raindrops hitting my windshield. I woke up when the car started rocking back and forth and realized we were having an earthquake.

Every run was like its own little chapter. By the end of the trip, I'd ridden in a propane truck, the town trash truck, and on a flatbed with a crane. I didn't care what kind of vehicle it was, as long as it took me to the top of the ski run.

V

I suppose you could say my wanderlust started when I was 3. I decided I was going to run away from home, so my mom packed me a small suitcase and watched as I walked to the end of the driveway and looked both ways. I kept looking both ways for a half-hour. Then I walked back up the driveway and sat down on our doorstep. The next time I ran away, I had found out that my next-door neighbors, Ramona and Harvey, were going to the beach with my babysitter, Patricia, who was their daughter. My mom said I couldn't go, so I snuck over to their house and climbed in their camper. Imagine their surprise when they got to the beach and found little Rainer had stowed away.

As an adult, if one adventure prepared me for the streak, it was a solo motorcycle ride up to Prudhoe Bay, Alaska, in the summer of 2003.

I have long been consumed by two means of overland travel: skiing and riding my motorcycle. The first time I rode a motorcycle, I was 9 years old. A friend who lived up on Sugarloaf Mountain above Boulder had two bikes, and we each rode one. The next year, my dad taught me to drive his Toyota Land Cruiser. (That led to mischief, like when I stole my mom's car and wrecked it when I was 15. Long story short, she had gone to Boulder and the three of us kids were left to run our family garage sale at home in the driveway. When I went to move my mom's Dodge Colt — the only new car she ever bought — I simply kept moving it. I picked up a couple of friends and we went for a joyride. Everything was fine until I took a corner too fast on Fish Creek Road. I rolled the car and totaled it. Luckily none of us got hurt, but as we were crawling out of the overturned car, a state patrolman walked up and said, "Can I see your driver's license?" I told him I didn't have one; he gave me a ticket and drove us home, where I burst into tears in front of my appalled mom.)

Now, I ride a BMW touring bike with cushy suspension for dirt roads yet still plenty of power for the open highway. The biggest benefit compared with a car or truck is better gas mileage, but the freedom and views are incredible too. If everyone rode bikes we wouldn't need so many major highway improvements and parking wouldn't be such a bitch everywhere. People would actually pay attention while driving, instead of texting or shaving or putting on lipstick.

The year before my Alaska trip, I took a "practice" trip to dial in my setup for the following summer. I wanted to test out the bike I'd just bought, as well as figure out what I'd need and what I wouldn't in the way of tools and gear. Earlier that season, I had the nail removed from my leg that I'd broken in 2001. They left it in for 18 months but didn't want it to grow into the bone, hence the extraction. My doctor wanted me to take it easy that summer, so naturally I asked if I could take a motorcycle trip.

"Just don't get your leg caught under the bike," he said. That was good enough for me.

I left Colorado in August and rode up to the Canadian border, through a bunch of national parks, over to the Pacific coast, then down to Lake Havasu and Flagstaff in Arizona, camping and visiting friends the whole way. I ended up riding about 9,000 miles, which only left me wanting more.

The next summer, after the 2002-'03 ski season ended, I set out for Prudhoe Bay. I started riding north in mid July — skied for a week on Mt. Hood to hit 4 million feet for the winter, visited a bunch of the San Juan Islands in Washington, then continued on to Vancouver Island. I caught a ferry from Port Hardy to Bella Coola, British Columbia, where I stayed with a dentist who knew my Uncle Adolf.

Bella Coola is one of the most gorgeous places in the world. The mountains jump out of the harbor and go straight up for 7,000 feet. They're glacier capped at the top. The only flatland in the area was around the river. I arrived just as the salmon run ended, unfortunately, so it was more like salmon-carcass season. I stayed there for a few days and got spooked riding on an old logging road when I came across a stretch dotted with bear soufflés. They were still steaming, which meant the bears that deposited them were probably nearby. I took that as a sign to skedaddle back to Bella Coola; when I got there I headed straight to the hardware store for bear bells. Usually people use bells to warn bears while they're hiking, but I figured since my ride is so quiet, they just might work for me too. After all, the provincial park I was going to be riding through supposedly has the highest-density bear population in the world.

I was kind of planning the trip as I went. I had a GPS to show me where I was and where the next town was, so I'd point my bike toward a place and see how it panned out. Plus, worst case, I had a tent so I figured I could find a place to sleep no matter what.

My rule was basically this: when you go by the last big town of the day, fill up with fuel, get something to eat, and find a place to camp. I didn't carry any food because I didn't want to bait bears. I had a flashlight and a fly rod, and I'd fill my hydration pack with water and stop at a liquor store to pick up a couple cans of beer or hard lemonade, then head off to camp and set up my two-man tent.

I met some hilarious characters along the way. I'm not a particularly outgoing person, but if someone wants to have a chat at a bar, I'm always up for it. That's all part of the pseudo survivalist you become when you're on an adventure: you have to ask questions, find out what's going on, where's the best place to camp, etc. I'd hold out my hand and say, "My name's Rainer. How ya doin'?"

From Bella Coola I rode to Prince Rupert, hopped on a ferry to Queen Charlotte Island, and started to explore the forest roads. I made it down to a beautiful bay on the west coast late that day, then camped at a trailhead near a small lake. The next morning I went for a hike and heard a crackling noise that sounded like a bear climbing a tree. I stopped for a bit and so did the noise; I took a few more steps and the noise started again. Suddenly, I heard a "crack, crack, boom!" A massive limb had broken off the tree and landed on the trail right in front of me. If I hadn't stopped, I would have been crushed and who knows how long it might have been until someone was there again.

After more bike touring, I returned to catch the ferry back to Prince Rupert. I had plenty of time to spare as I neared the town, so I slowed down to about 20 mph to enjoy the scenery. Suddenly a bald eagle flew out of the woods and began hovering alongside my bike, about an arm's length from my fuel tank. It was unlike anything I've ever experienced. I was looking at the bird's eyeballs; he was flying at the same speed I was riding my bike. He stayed next to me for a hundred yards or so, then darted back into the woods, apparently having gotten his thrill for the day.

From Prince Rupert I ferry-hopped up the coast, stopping in Ketchikan on my way to Juneau, the Alaska state capital. One day was all it took to see every road in Juneau, so I headed up to Haines in search of an old friend named Greg. I knew Greg and his twin brother, B, from growing up in Estes Park, and I talked to B before I left Colorado.

"I've been up there," B told me, "and if you walk around town at 6 p.m., Greg's either in this bar or this bar or this bar. If you don't find him there, he's at home or working."

I took his advice and asked around. Haines is a small town; everybody knows everybody. The bartender at one of the places Greg frequents told me he'd be in shortly. I hung out and had something to eat, and sure enough, Greg walked in the door an hour later.

We caught up over beers then I stayed at his cabin that night. He'd had a bad experience with a bear — he opened his front door after cooking dinner one night, and a grizzly was standing there insistent that Greg let him in for leftovers — so he cut a hole in his ceiling and began sleeping in his attic, which he accessed with a ladder. He gave me the couch on the main level, which was not the safest-feeling place to sleep, but I lived.

I rode from Haines back into Canada and up to Whitehorse, the capital of the Yukon Territory, where I crashed with a couple I'd met in Haines named Miles and Kim. Miles told me about an old gold-mining town called Atlin and said the fishing for arctic grayling there was off the charts — incredibly aggressive fish that attack your hook like piranhas. To prove it, he told me one day he and his son were going fishing, and the kid's hook was dangling from his pack as they walked over a bridge. A fish leaped up and swallowed the hook in midair. So he caught a fish without even fishing! Kim didn't believe him when he told her the story, but a few weeks later they were going out to camp in the same location, and Kim was carrying her pole the same way their son had. Sure enough, a fish jumped out of the water and swallowed her hook too.

I couldn't resist seeing for myself, so I stopped in Atlin and took a rest day to do some fishing. He hadn't exaggerated the grayling's aggressiveness at all. I was using a fly rod and a mosquito, and there were times when the fish was on my hook before it even hit the water. After two hours of casting in the same spot, I quit because my hands were so cold from taking fish off my hook.

On my way north, people often asked me, "Why do you want to go to Prudhoe Bay? Once you get over the pass, nothing grows, not even trees. It's all just a tundra wasteland."

I'd say, "That's what I want to see. I want to see where the trees end."

From Whitehorse, I set out for Dawson City, where you can do a shot with a frozen toe in it. You actually have to take the toe into your mouth, somebody's frozen toe, then spit it back into the shot glass. I didn't partake in that, but I found a road up to the top of a little mountain where you can see the whole town. I pitched my tent up there; when I woke up in the morning, the whole valley was obscured by clouds, but I was in the sunshine. It felt surreal.

I took a ferry across the Yukon River and headed toward Top of the World Highway and back into Alaska, one of the most scenic drives in North America. The border control up there is pretty hilarious. It's a tiny little cabin with an American flag. The guy walks out and looks at your passport, then says, "Go ahead!" I asked him, "Do you mind if I take a picture of this?" He didn't mind.

Five hours west of Dawson City is a funky little town called

Chicken, Alaska. There are a few small cabins, one of which is a bar where they claim to have the biggest hat collection in the world. There are hats on top of hats on top of hats, hanging from the ceiling, from the walls, everywhere. There's also a general store and, of course, a liquor store. It's where people go to hunt and fish and pan for gold.

From Chicken, I headed to Eagle and saw something I'd never seen before: A dogsled team pulling its musher down the street on an ATV. I asked the guy, whose name was Bob, what they were doing, and he said the dogs were training for the Iditarod.

My next stop was Circle. I was sitting in a bar downtown when a local guy sat down next to me and introduced himself as John Brown. "I'm a gold miner," he said, then he launched into a fascinating explanation about how he gets his gold.

When the Yukon River freezes solid, he essentially mines the river bottom. He uses front-end loaders and dump trucks that are about four feet tall, pulls silt out from under the ice, then in the summer he runs it through a screen and extracts the gold. It's pretty bizarre, but he has mining claims on the river bottom, so he's dialed. He always mines the same spot because all the gold ends up flowing into that hole, he said. Some of the chunks of gold he showed me were as big as grapes.

As we were leaving, he said he liked my BMW motorcycle and pulled up next to me on his bike. It was a really old vintage BMW with the sidecar attached like they used in World War 2. His wife had one too.

I rode through Fairbanks, which qualifies as a big city for interior Alaska, and continued north toward Prudhoe Bay. Just after you cross the Yukon River on the Dawson Highway, you pass through a little knick-knack stop called the Arctic Circle. It's actually a bit south of the actual latitude, but you can still buy a shirt that says, "Congratulations, you've made it to the Arctic Circle!"

From there the road surface varies between pavement and dirt. The road grader rips apart the dirt that time of year and exposes all the rocks, so whenever I found myself between paved sections, I was riding over loose, sharp, gnarly terrain that could have easily punctured a tire. Simply riding 10 miles sapped my energy and felt like 100 miles because of the stress.

What I learned riding the rough surface is inside every big pot hole are seven little ones. At 35 mph, you hit every single divot. At 50, you skip some little ones, and at 70, you fly from big pot hole to big pot hole and don't even feel the little ones. But if you wreck at 70, it could be your last day on the planet. I went 70 anyway because the quality of the ride was so much better. You just take your chances and go.

I wasn't sure how far I had to ride from Arctic Circle to Prudhoe Bay, and I was starting to run low on fuel. Suddenly I came upon a guy sitting in his car taking photos of something in the road. As I went to ride around him, I saw a giant grizzly bear standing in our way. It started walking toward one side of the road, so even though my yellow fuel light was on, I gunned it past him on the opposite edge and kept going. Sure enough, a mile after I passed the bear, I ran out of fuel. Luckily I had a two-gallon can of gas that a concerned bartender had given me outside Fairbanks a few days earlier. I dumped it in my bike and made it to Prudhoe Bay with ease from there.

The scene near Prudhoe Bay is almost prehistoric. You can see the Gates of the Arctic National Park, as well as the tall peaks on the upper end of the Yukon. I also watched a herd of musk ox wander around the barren tundra, their shaggy hair and big horns evoking images of the long extinct wooly mammoth. The landscape was desolate and flat, but it was also really unique in that sense. And ironic, considering you're on a road that leads to the biggest oil pipeline in the world.

When I asked about a hotel room, the receptionist quoted me $150 for their crappiest room. I wasn't about to pay that, so I ate some food, fueled up and filled my gas can, then started heading south. It was not unlike a trip up Mt. Everest in that sense: You spend weeks getting to the summit, then you're only there for a half-hour before you start the long trip home. But, as they say, the summit is only a destination; the journey is the true reward.

The leaves and tundra had begun changing colors along Top

of the World Highway, and the rest of the ride was even more colorful and gorgeous. Being on the bike was like walking through it all, except I was covering more ground.

At one point during my ride I saw a purple ptarmigan, which is really rare. Ptarmigan reflect their surroundings, and up in Alaska, the tundra turns purple in the fall. I would never have seen this one except that it was standing in the middle of the road.

The ride back from Prudhoe Bay was as rugged and dusty as the ride up. Just my luck, I ended up behind a car that had two boats tied to it with crappy twine string. The driver would not let me past no matter what I did; I think he wanted me to eat his dust for 200 miles. When I finally saw a window to pass him, I flew by so fast that he didn't even know I had.

I got to the tiny town of Coldfoot (population: 10) after going over Atigun Pass, and stopped to get gas and something to eat. As I was walking out of the restaurant, here comes this old guy with his two grandkids, and he starts giving me hell.

"You drive like that, son? I'm a retired police officer and I'll throw you in jail!"

"Who the hell are you?" I said.

"You went past me 200 miles back there, you sumbitch! I've seen a motorcycle rider with his head gone through a moose!"

"Well, I grew up where there's deer and elk everywhere so I know to look out for them. Sorry you feel that way."

"You smartass sumbitch," he shot back. "I know a big old German cop who would kick your ass!"

I felt like saying, "Which part of 'you're retired' do you not understand?" I didn't get into how his load looked really shaky and why didn't he just let me by him in the first place. Instead I just shrugged it off and got on my bike and left.

On my way back through Fairbanks, I rode out to Chena Hot Springs, a small resort that has been rejuvenating weary travelers for more than 100 years. It was pouring rain at the time so I didn't want to pitch my tent (in two months on the road, I spent about seven nights in motels or the like, simply to dry out my drenched gear from all the rain I encountered). I rented a yurt for $20 and soaked my weary bones and muscles in the hot springs for hours on end. It felt like someone was warming up my soul.

I got to talking with a local and he told me how happy he is to live in Alaska, where you can ride your ATV anywhere you want and don't have to deal with people bothering you; you can just deal with the consequences of your actions. It made me think about the many levels of freedom in our country, and reminded me to be grateful for what I have, even if it's not quite as loose as that guy's version of freedom.

At breakfast the next morning, as I was paying my bill, the manager said, "Hey, you're that fella on the motorcycle, right?" When I told him I was, he said, "You might want to think about getting out of here. The Chena River is starting to flood over the highway back toward Fairbanks. You could be stranded here for a week."

My first thought was it wouldn't be a bad place to be stranded for a week. But I had a long way to go before I got home to Colorado, and I didn't want to take that chance. So I hopped on my bike and raced back toward Fairbanks.

Sure enough, when I reached the river, it was already over the highway. Fording it looked daunting. I watched a few cars and trucks go through, and I saw where it was shallowest. I figured I might as well try to get across.

Fording a river on a motorcycle is like riding into a strong sidewind. You have to lean into the current and hope. I made it across, but realized I may have taken on water through a breather hole on the back drive unit. I decided I'd get the bike serviced in Fairbanks, which I needed to do anyway, having ridden 7,000 miles since my last oil change and valve adjustment.

The Fairbanks BMW shop is way back in the woods. To get there, you ride a singletrack through the forest. The shop is staffed by one guy who not only services bikes but also collects vintage BMWs, Mercedes, and other motorcycles, some of which I'd never heard of. He has three cabins on the property: the first is where he lives, stores parts, and does his office work; the second is where he does oil changes and other basic repairs; and the third is where he builds machinery and stores his vintage bikes.

My buddy Greg had told me in Haines that you have to watch what you leave in your yard in Alaska, because if you leave stuff sitting around for too long, the flora will actually grow over it and you'll never find it again. It really is that aggressive. I finally saw what he meant at the Fairbanks BMW shop. An entire fleet of old Mercedes was in danger of disappearing forever.

The mechanic was quite the character. Well into his 60s if not his early 70s, he told me when he first got to Alaska, he and two other guys ran bulldozers and built the first road up to Prudhoe Bay. He was amazing to talk to, and his shop was unlike anything I'd ever seen. The fronts of the cabins were solid and the siding made it look like they were full buildings, but the backs of the cabins had no wall whatsoever; they were open-air. Not that anyone could steal anything even if they wanted to. The forest was so thick that it would be impossible to escape.

I ogled Denali — the highest mountain in North America at 20,237 feet — on my way south then turned west and rode the Denali Highway. It was similar to the Dawson Highway in that there were paved sections as well as sections where the grader was busy ripping up the road. I stopped to see Tim Crowley, a high school buddy, and his wife in Eagle Creek, then I tried to look up a friend from Breckenridge who had moved to Girdwood. No luck, but when I was in the Girdwood bike shop, I noticed a pair of Rainier skis hanging on the wall. I asked the owner if they were for sale, since finding anything that has any resemblance to my name is rare. The price tag said $9.99 but he wanted $100. I said OK if he paid shipping; he agreed, and lo and behold, they were at home when I got back.

I rode through the tunnel to Seward then on to Soldotna to visit some friends on the Kenai Peninsula. From Soldotna I headed south and caught the ferry from Homer to Kodiak. This vessel was the first ship to run the Alaska Highway, which is what they call the ferry service from the lower 48 to Alaska and back. As you board the ship, you drive onto a turntable that spins 90 degrees as it drops down into the bowels of the ship. Strap the bike down and away you go, chugging through the crater of an extinct volcano on your way out to Kodiak Island.

While I was on the boat, I met a guy who tests outdoor gear for the U.S. military. The guy brought up Kodiak bears. "You got a gun, dontcha?" he asked. "No, why?" I said. He told me that Kodiak bears are the biggest bears in the world. "They grow to 14, 15 feet tall."

I told him I had bear spray. He laughed. "That's just like pepper to those bears, they lick their lips and you taste better that way!"

Now I was scared. While camping on the island I parked my bike in front of my tent, so if a bear ever came to get me, he'd knock over the bike first. I knew it wouldn't stop him, but at least I'd know he was there.

I didn't see any Kodiak bears, but I toured every road on the island in one day, and saw the biggest buffalo of my life. The animal was way out in a field and looked to be eight to 10 feet tall standing on all fours — easily. It blew my mind. I also saw a creek so full of salmon you couldn't see any water; all you could see was fish. That's when I figured, there has to be a bear around here somewhere, which means I should skedaddle once again. I caught the last ferry that night since I was told that if I didn't, it would be a week before the next one came.

I caught up with a guy in Anchorage, Chris Backstrum, whom I'd grown up with in Estes Park and hadn't seen for 20 years. He confided that he was a bit nervous to see me. I asked why and he told me that he'd nailed me with a snowball when we were kids and felt guilty about it ever since. We laughed. I remembered the incident but never knew who hit me and had long ago put my ire out to pasture. But it was still funny to hear something like that at our age.

The first snowstorm of the season hit soon after I left Anchorage. It was miserable. I rode through 200 miles of snow from Whitehorse down the Cassiar Highway and was completely frozen by the time I stopped to get a hotel room. The next morning brought more snow, but it cleared up as I finally neared the end of the highway. I thought I was home free. I was wrong.

The government was paving the road in advance of winter, and unlike warm-weather roads, their pavement has a lot of small, sharp rocks mixed in to help with traction during the frozen months. When I stopped for fuel I examined my already worn-out tires, and saw they were full of sharp rocks embedded in the rubber. I spent a half-hour plucking rocks out of the tires before continuing south. I also called ahead and ordered new tires from a bike shop in Prince George. They were backed up with work orders but said if I pulled the wheels off myself, they could fit me in. While in the shop, I also bought a heated vest to keep me warm the next time I rode through a snowstorm.

In southern B.C., I passed through Kamloops and stopped in Whistler, home to what many believe is the best ski area in the world. Since the resort was owned by the same company that owns Copper, they hooked me up with a free gondola pass and I toured their snowcat maintenance shop. From Whistler I continued on to my cousin's house in Seattle, and then, at long last, home to Colorado.

All told, I rode 17,500 miles in two months, not counting my 14 ferry rides. The trip opened my eyes to the world, as every true adventure does.

VI

That motorcycle trip remains a defining event in my life, but in actuality, it was just a precursor to *the* defining event.

Although my streak gained steam in the first two years, it accelerated in Year 3 thanks to a handful of affirming occasions, some measurable, some not. Most interesting to the world at large, 2006 was the year I passed 1,000 consecutive days. This led to stories and photos in Outside Magazine, on CNN, and in a host of newspapers — including The New York Times — thanks to a feature by the Associated Press.

Most gratifying to me, it was also the year I set my personal record for most vertical skied in a day: 115,395 feet on March 29, 2006 — two months after I skied the deepest snow I've ever skied.

It didn't take much to keep me motivated, but a fortuitous trip back to Jackson Hole in late January — the dog days of winter, when the sun hangs low in the sky and the nights are long and frigid — recharged my battery at just the right time.

My old buddy KZ, short for Kevin Zurfluh, had some work to take care of near Jackson. KZ and I are friends from back in Estes Park; he's been one of my most trusted ski partners for more than 35 years. He works as a systems technician for the federal government, and his bosses asked him to drive up to Grand Teton National Park and do some radio communications repair. He asked if I wanted to go, and initially I declined. I was so focused on my goal at Copper that I worried I'd miss a day or that I wouldn't get as much vertical if

I traveled out of state. Luckily, KZ persisted.

"Don't worry, Rainer. I'll get you there. I'll get you back. You won't miss a day," he promised.

So along with another friend of ours, Bill Halogen, we made the eight-hour drive up to Jackson on January 25, after I skied for an hour at Copper to record the day. Once there we met up with Kevin Coughlan, another old bud from Estes, who worked at the resort and still skied in leather telemark boots (his attitude was, "If you're skiing in plastic, you ain't shit!"). The four of us made a ski weekend out of KZ's work trip; I called it "my ski vacation from my ski life."

Our first morning in Jackson, we lucked into early access passes that got us on the hill before the lifts opened to the public. They're called "locker passes," and to get one, you pay extra for your season pass then get to board the lifts early with the lifties and ski patrol. You have a locker at the top so you can change into your ski gear, eat a donut, and wait for patrol to finish its avalanche mitigation. Once that happens, you're cleared to go get first tracks.

After an incredible first run, we went for another lap on the same lift since the first guests were just starting to show up. We bumped into a patroller at the top of the lift who was hiking up to the Headwall. I looked at KZ. "Shit, man, we ought to follow this guy, he looks like he knows where to go." The patroller heard me and said, "Are you friends of Kevin's?" We nodded. "I'm the guy who got Kevin to move here from Alta. I'll show you where to go."

We hiked up the Headwall, and suddenly he stopped. "Everyone keeps going straight here. They just follow each other like lemmings. Take a right, walk over to the end of that cornice, and ski down that ridge line. You'll have the best run of your life."

He wasn't kidding. KZ and I put on our skis and looked at each other. There was no "You go first" or "No, you go first," we just took off and skied down side by side. You could see everything you were doing, you just couldn't breathe, because the snow was up to our goggles. It was total flotation, like tunneling through bottomless goose feathers. We finally got down to the catwalk and this guy who was traversing across skied up to us. "Wow," he said. "That's the coolest thing I've ever seen."

We continued to hit it hard from open to close. KZ left me to ski all the steep lines out of bounds, and I hammered vertical inbounds.

Cooked like game hens and thirsty like sailors, we stumbled into the Mangy Moose for an après ski session. Live music echoed through the spacious saloon, and everyone was buzzing from the epic powder day. Still in our ski boots, soaked by sweat and snow, we ended up sitting at a table right below the 6 Million Club plaque. Kevin knew more than we did about the club, since he lived in Jackson and worked at the resort, so he gave us more background about its members. I wished I could have told the members about the numbers I was hitting, but it didn't matter.

I was still hungry to ski after our après session, so I went over to Snow King — a small ski area in downtown Jackson that offers night skiing — and skied until they closed. I recorded 77,000 vertical feet that day over nine hours and 15 minutes, by far my biggest day on snow at the time. I remember skiing my last run at Snow King and continuing toward where I thought Kevin's backyard was. I missed it by a block but kept skiing into a four-way-stop intersection since there was so much snow on the ground. Just my luck, though, I hit a patch where it had melted down to gravel and my skis stopped cold, catapulting my body onto the street in a brutal faceplant. All the cars at the intersection had stopped to let me ski through, which made it even more humbling. I was almost too tired to laugh.

We had a hell of a time that trip, skiing hard, staying up late, feeling younger than we were. I was sad it had to end, but the rest of my winter awaited me at Copper, and I was eager to resume my vertical assault at home.

***

Ripping downhill through powder is typically the best part of any skier's winter, but for me it was always a Catch 22. I'm a ski bum at heart, and I love fresh snow just as much as the next guy. But in a good winter — and the 2005-06 season started out in epic fashion, with more than seven feet of snow in November, then continued at a steady pace — when I ski day after day of chopped-up powder, my legs feel like porridge. It kind of takes the fun out of it, especially when you never have a rest day to let your muscles heal.

Even if I just had two or three days of packed snow, it would change how I felt a lot, because my legs didn't have to work as hard to keep me in control on the way down. That winter, as strange as it sounds, powder was dampening my spirit because I was sore all the time. I never thought I'd feel so much mental anguish getting out of bed on a powder day.

That said, there's a difference between chopped-up powder and untracked powder. It's kind of like water skiing on glass versus on a white-capped lake. It's a lot more fun to ski on glass.

There were a number of days when I sacrificed vertical because the snow was that good. I went and skied my secret stashes, which really cuts down on the vert you're able to ski on groomers. But I was still getting close to my numbers, and it was well worth it. At one secret spot, I had four sets of figure eights lined up side by side before anyone else showed up. It's a spot you can ski to really easily, but people always drop in before they get there.

In late March, I decided to maximize a day more than I ever had before. Keystone was running its lifts at night to please the spring break crowds, so I showed up just after they opened at 8:30 a.m. and didn't stop skiing until they closed at 9 that night.

A 75-year-old mother of five was aiming to ski 75,000 vertical feet on her birthday the same day. Her name was Freda Langell Nieters, and as female skiers go in Summit County, she's the queen. She raced for the Norwegian national team in the 1940s, then won an NCAA championship in 1951. She was one of the first instructors Keystone hired when it opened in 1970. In 2009, she was inducted into the Colorado Ski and Snowboard Hall of Fame.

Freda lost a grandson to Sudden Infant Death Syndrome (SIDS), so she used her 75th birthday as an excuse to go big and raise a bunch of money for SIDS research. I ended up skiing 40,000 feet more than Freda that day, but my plight wasn't nearly as noble.

The day started ominously when I wiped out in the parking lot on a patch of ice. It got better when I picked up a comp ticket courtesy of Chuck Tolton, who used to be the patrol director at Copper and went on to be the head of skier safety for Vail Resorts. Chuck was happy to assist my streak, and I was happy he did.

Twelve hours is a long time to ski, and the conditions reflected that. I started out on frozen corduroy, which turned into four inches of slush, which refroze after sunset, at which point four inches of powder fell and freshened everything up. I got a bit of a bonus when the lifties — surely carrying out a kind gesture from Chuck — told me I could use the patrol lane, which made my turnaround times a few minutes quicker.

I skied pretty much nonstop save for two diversions. When I passed 30 million vertical feet for my streak, I stopped on the hill, cracked open a beer, and thanked all of my guardian angels and deceased ski friends for looking out for me. I also took a couple of laps on the beginner run at the top of the mountain to say goodbye to my friend Toad. Toad and I had done the dirt work to shape the trails and areas where the lift terminals were installed. Toad passed away in a motorcycle accident the previous fall, and I wanted to remember our times together at Keystone.

After 12 hours and eight minutes of skiing, I limped back to my car to find out I'd left my parking lights on. I needed a jump to start my car, which was about how my body felt too.

On May 18 that year, I drove to A-Basin to meet a photographer from Outside Magazine, Lisa Wyatt, for my first real photo shoot. I got there at 6 a.m. and proceeded to pose in all sorts of crazy ways, befitting my crazy streak. She had me sit in a beach chair and punch snowballs as she threw them at me one by one, then I got towed behind a snowmobile with a beer in one hand and my poles in another. They used a full-page shot of me standing among some trees with suspenders on, looking up at the Continental Divide. The headline for the story was "Rainer Shine."

A few months later, at Mt. Hood, I celebrated my 1,000th consecutive ski day (which also would've been my grandmother's 99th birthday) at Charlie's. My favorite bartender, Geoff Ecker, may he rest in peace, chilled a Crown Royal to perfection. It was so cold the ice was frozen onto the glass.

In mid-August, a huge monarch butterfly migration took over Mt. Hood. At times they were so thick you couldn't avoid them. I'd get to the bottom of a run, and I'd be wearing a bunch of butterflies on my clothes. It was unlike anything I'd ever seen.

I found out that they normally migrate through a different area on Mt. Hood, but due to a big wildfire on the east side of the volcano, they changed course and flew up the Palmer Snowfield. It lasted a week or so. They migrated for two or three hours a day, and they'd be gone by the time I started grooming in late afternoon. If you skied at just the right speed, you were perfectly in sync with them and they were able to avoid you. If you went too fast, they splattered on you. They would stop to drink water at the edge of the snowfield, where it melts on the warm lava, then continue their journey. I called it tele'ing in a butterfly blizzard.

As a reminder of just how wild nature can be, four days after the butterfly migration began, I witnessed an enormous rockslide up high. Ten boulders the size of cars ripped free from the mountain and rumbled downhill, thankfully in an unpopulated area. I watched one of the rocks bounce 200 feet in the air, it was going so fast.

In South America that year, I skied 15 different resorts between Argentina and Chile, mostly trying to build up what I called my Slush Fund. While attempting to maintain a pace of 1 million vertical feet per month, I often ran into times when I simply couldn't ski as much as I wanted. Sometimes it was weather related, sometimes the lifts broke down, sometimes I was traveling. But every day that I skied less than 33,000 vertical feet essentially put me behind schedule and left me in a bad mood, because I felt like I failed that day.

To combat that, I'd try to accumulate extra vert whenever I could, and my annual South America trips were the perfect time to do that. Of course, once all the resorts closed, I still had to ski each day, and maximizing my hitchhike laps was the only way to soften the blow to my Slush Fund. Near the end of my trip in October 2006, I hitchhike-skied 10 days in a row. The locals took to calling me "Gringo Loco de Guinness," which I took as a compliment.

I got picked up that year by an 85-year-old man and his grandson, a helicopter ski guide, four ladies from Michigan in their van, and a pair of brothers from Brazil. On my last day I skied in shorts with no shirt, then posed for a photo with a hot Chilean girl who thought I looked cool.

I flew home to Colorado on October 21 and was treated to a 15-inch powder day at Loveland the next morning. It felt like Ullr was saying, "Welcome back, Rainer!"

I passed three years of daily skiing on Halloween, of course, skiing 36 runs at Copper then 10 runs at Loveland and five at A-Basin. After finishing at the Basin, I ducked into the A-frame base lodge for a celebratory cocktail at the 6th Alley Bar. I caught a ride home and kept celebrating deep into the night, which led to a foggy start to Year 4.

Photographer Marc Piscotty took this shot of me skiing at Copper Mountain in 2006. I had just passed three years of daily skiing.

VII

In mid-November 2006, a reporter from the Rocky Mountain News, James Meadow, drove up to Copper to report a feature on my streak (9News had done a story the prior week). He wasn't a skier, so he met me after I'd finished for the day. He was expecting me to be beat up and tired from skiing 33,000 vertical feet. He couldn't believe that I was happy.

I was in a rush, trying to cook my meal, get changed and get to work, but he came out and rode with me in the snowcat for a while, so he really got to see what my day-to-day routine was like, minus the skiing. "The World's Greatest Ski Bum," he called me in his story. I told him I still felt like a kid — with 45 years of experience.

One of the most memorable days from my streak happened three days after my meeting with Meadow, and had little to do with skiing. My mom — Gisela Hertrich — was scheduled to marry her longtime boyfriend, a lovable Brit named Peter Daniels, and I wanted to do something cool for their wedding. I called my buddy Raul at Stage Coach Limousines and arranged for a limo to pick up my family, then stop and pick me up on their way to the wedding, which was to take place the afternoon of November 19 at the Copper Chapel.

I had already skied my vert for the day and was sitting in the hot tub with my friend Rudi, when it occurred to me that I could actually ski to my mom's wedding. I hustled into my condo, put on my suit, then headed over to the chairlift. I saw some friends in line who were confused. "What are you doing in a suit, Rainer?"

I rode the Excelerator lift to the top of Copper and skied all the way down to the road, where the limo would be passing through. I made it just as the driver pulled up to the Athletic Club. He walked across the street, grabbed my skis, and carried them over to the stretch limo. I climbed in with my poles in my hand, and almost laughed out loud at some of the looks I got during our 100-yard ride to the Chapel.

At the wedding, as I walked my mom down the aisle and gave her away to Peter, no one saw that I was wearing my ski boots. It left me smiling inside. And my boots were much more comfortable than my dress shoes.

My mom has an incredible story of her own. Long before I was born, she and her family suffered the indignity and bad timing of living in Germany during World War 2. She was born in 1937 in Wanne-Eickel, which later got integrated with a larger city called Herne. Not long after the war began, Wanne-Eickel started getting bombed on a regular basis. My mom and her brother, as well as their parents, would rush into a bunker below their house for shelter. Her dad got them in first, then he grabbed some wet towels so that when they climbed out of the bunker, they could protect themselves from the burning embers that were falling from the sky. The embers burned a lot of people in her city.

She and her family moved to a farm near Hannover that belonged to her dad's family. They lived there until the war ended, along with her grandfather, her uncle and some cousins. "That's what you did during the war," she says. "You went *somewhere*."

They baked bread, farmed potatoes, made hay. Cows, pigs, chickens, and rabbits roamed their land. Beginning when she was five years old, she walked every morning to a one-room schoolhouse nearby; in high school, she walked 20 minutes to a train station then rode the rails for a half-hour to the closest girls' high school.

If you ask her what the war was like, she'll say, "I know that it was miserable and I know that lots of people died who shouldn't have, and I know that the Nazis were bastards, pardon me. And I know that my dad was taken off the street to Siberia the day that the war was over, and he died of starvation in Siberia."

Her father was a high-school teacher, and this is the story she was told as a child. The day before the war ended in 1945, he took his students — who were on summer vacation at the time, but he did this every summer — to a bunkhouse for a little getaway east of where we lived. When they were leaving the bunkhouse to return home, all the kids had boarded the bus and he was double checking the building to make sure everything was locked up. That's when the Russians swooped in and took him off the street, never to be seen again.

It was probably because they knew the war was ending and they wanted to take as many last-minute prisoners as they could. "Heaven only knows," my mom says. "The Russians were assholes!"

My grandmother told me the story a few times when I was little, kind of like, "This is why you never met Grandpa."

My grandfather on my dad's side, meanwhile, was a priest. He would say, "I work for God," and that was something Hitler and the Nazis did not mess with. He also said it to protect my dad and his brothers, Adolf (who lives in Oregon) and Walter (who passed away two years ago in Munich). By saying he needed his sons for the church, he hoped the Nazis would leave them alone. And they did. They ended up in Donauwörth and my grandfather lived there until his death.

***

Despite all the logistics it took to keep my streak running smoothly, easily the most remarkable part, in my opinion, was the fact that I never got injured. I got hurt, don't get me wrong (if you've ever skied with a separated shoulder or bruised ribs, you know how agonizing it is), and ill (one day I called in sick due to the flu but still went skiing for two hours to feed the streak), but never injured to the point of not being able to ski.

Ironically, and I still think about it to this day, one of the closest calls I had with injury happened off the snow. After a January day at Copper when I skied Drainpipe in waist-deep powder, I decided to treat myself to a celebratory T-bone steak. I had it on the grill and was walking out to get it from the deck. One of the wooden steps was completely glazed by ice. My feet slipped out from under me and I fell flat on my back and hips. It felt like a wrecking ball smashed the middle of my body. I still don't know how I managed to hold on to the plate.

The next morning was almost the end of the streak. Searing pain coursed through my back and down to my knee. There was no way I was going skiing.

Then I thought about it some more and decided I couldn't quit over a barbecue mishap. I got out of bed, took a shot of Crown, two Aleves and three Bayers, and hobbled out the door to go skiing. Even riding the lift put me in agony, but I made it through a few runs and actually felt better when I finished than I did when I started. Funny how physical activity does that to the body sometimes. And drugs.

The pain gradually subsided in the ski days that followed — I put all the weight on my good side when I turned, a trick I learned when I broke my leg as a kid and skied on one ski — until I was back to skiing pain free.

Stories like that are why, whenever someone asked me, "What's your goal?" my first response was always, "Tomorrow."

In June 2007, I skied until the Summit County lift-served season ended once again (A-Basin's staff was nice enough to buy me lunch on my birthday), then headed down to Estes Park and back to my roots. I hiked for turns at Hidden Valley, which is now a ghost ski area, and on my second day there I met a guy named Lee who had skied at least one day a month for 151 consecutive months. For all I know, his streak could still be alive.

My trip to Oregon again took me through Utah and Idaho, where I crawled over logs and branches to reach the snow with my buddy Smoothy, my 11th straight day hiking for turns. I was always happy to get back to Timberline and the Palmer Snowfield. By this time — my fourth summer there — I felt at home. The lifties handed me slices of pizza to keep me going on hot days. I knew most of the regulars at Charlie's, and let me tell you, there were some characters to know. One guy we called Dirty Carl. He put the bum in ski bum. He would trade cocktails for cleaning up somebody's puke in the bathroom — that's how he got his nickname.

He didn't ski much because he couldn't afford it, but every summer a nice couple he was friends with named Nic and Ann would fly to Oregon and take him skiing for a week. Those were really the only times I saw him on the hill.

Probably the most famous of my friends at Timberline was a guy we call Fuxi. Fuxi's real name is Franz Fuchsberger. He's 56 but thinks he's 26. He grew up in Austria, came to the U.S. in 1983 and won the Powder 8 world championship six times. Now he lives in Edwards, Colorado, 45 minutes west of Copper, and sells loudly colored ski-racing suits and other accessories to kids who think they're going to be the next Bode Miller — or masters racers who wish they had been. Every summer from May to September, he plants himself at Mt. Hood, promotes his business, and skis. He's still a hot skier, and he can sell anything to anybody.

Fuxi used to joke that if I ever took a day off from skiing and didn't tell anyone, he'd be the first to know. Truth be told, the thought actually crossed my mind that I could maybe do that, especially on the super rainy days in Oregon. But so many people were keeping an eye on me that I'm convinced someone would've noticed if I didn't ski. My skis would've still been in my locker, for one. And if I didn't show up, since I was living in a tent, I would've been downtown in the bar all day, because I wasn't going to sit in my tent in the rain. It would've been pretty obvious if I didn't go.

But that didn't keep Fuxi from fancying himself a watchdog. One day he was up skiing in the clouds at Timberline and it got to be late in the day; since we hadn't crossed paths yet he figured I might be trying to weasel out of skiing. He was all excited to bust me, then he saw me poke through the fog coming down the run while he was on the lift. He recognized me immediately because he knows the way I turn. "Raiiiiiiinerrrrrrrr!" he bellowed from the lift. I always loved seeing Fuxi on the mountain.

After my predawn run on September 4, I flew back to Chile and bummed around the Andes for the fourth year in a row. I preferred traveling around to different ski areas as opposed to staying in one place. I'd put all my expenses on my Visa. I figured, I'm doing this once, and whatever it costs is what I'm going to pay. Some of the ski areas were $65 a day, others were less than $20. To cut down on costs, sometimes I'd arrive to a new resort late at night, sleep in my car, then get up and go skiing.

For the most part I went wherever I could get the most vertical for my time. Valle Nevado, La Parva, El Colorado, and Nevados de Chillan — which was surrounded by mineral hot springs — were the best Chilean resorts for vert. I could ski 60,000-foot days at Valle Nevado pretty easily, which helped me build my Slush Fund. By comparison, when I returned to Colorado, it took me all day, going as hard and fast as I could, to reach 50,000 feet at Loveland.

In Argentina, Las Leñas and Bariloche were pricey, but Caviahue, Los Penitentes, and La Hoya were fun little affordable ski areas that allowed me to hit my numbers, even if it took most of the day.

The only problem with traveling a lot was it left me vulnerable to logistical breakdowns. One day, on my way to Cerro Bayo, I drove through a national park and a long stretch of dirt roads that were so wet they'd turned to mud. At first it was passable, then the mud got thick and the trenches grew deeper.

I wasn't sure if I'd make it through. The car was barely running. When I finally got to the other side, there was so much mud in the engine that I couldn't believe it was still on. The hotel I checked into let me hose off the inside of the engine, then I took the car to a garage the next day and had them rinse it out so I wouldn't get in trouble when I returned it.

At the end of my 2007 stay in South America, I again strung together some hiking and hitchhiking days near Valle Nevado. Hitchhiking for turns always signals the end of a season for me, and when the snow melts in Chile, I start pining for Colorado where winter is just beginning. I flew home from Santiago and got picked up at the airport by Ginger, "my favorite spice," whom I hadn't seen in nearly five months.

VIII

A lot of people played important roles in my streak, but among that broader group, a few were crucial. Ginger was one of them. From encouraging Guinness to recognize my new (and ongoing) record to supporting me both in person and from afar, it made a big difference to know the streak was even remotely as important to someone else as it was to me.

Ginger and I met in 2002 in Estes Park. We were in what used to be my favorite bar in town, Lonigans. It was a packed Friday night in the heart of summer, right before the Fourth of July, when Estes goes from a sleepy little hamlet to a tourist trap with people everywhere. That night happened to be Ginger's birthday. I walked in the back door and immediately noticed her at the bar, sitting two chairs away from the waitress stand. That's a good-looking babe, I thought, and asked if she'd mind if I took a seat next to her. "Go ahead," she said.

She told me later that her first impression of me had been, "This guy's trouble," but apparently she liked trouble. It helped that she thought I was attractive too, and we drank and danced the night away. At the end of the night she invited me to her hotel room. We had a blast for the next couple of days, but like many good things, it came with a caveat. "I'm glad I met you, and I hate to tell you this," I said, "but I'm leaving for Alaska tomorrow on my motorcycle." The next morning I set out for Prudhoe Bay.

I called her a couple of times during the two months I was on the road, which surprised her; she thought I was gone forever. When I got back I called her again to see if she was still interested. Indeed she was. She invited me to her house in Denver and we had another memorable night. We started seeing each other pretty regularly after that.

She was working for a satellite TV company when we met, then she lost her job and her cat got diabetes and her mother was dying. I was a good escape for her, and she was good for me. I appreciated her company. Of course, it didn't make our relationship easy that my streak began shortly after we got together. But we made it work for seven years.

Ginger came from a communications family — her father published a newspaper in suburban Boston, where she grew up, and her mother worked in PR. She was a ski photographer in Vermont for 15 years before she moved to Colorado, and she shared her parents' love of spreading news and sparking people's interest about unusual things. Which worked out well for me and my streak, because she helped get the word out to media and places that I never would've reached otherwise.

She was the first to contact Guinness and tell them what I was doing. When they said they didn't have a category for anything related to telemark skiing, she helped them understand it enough that they created one specifically for me and my pursuit. (Imagine trying to explain that to someone who had never skied: "Free your heel, free your mind, dude. What don't you understand?") Later, she contacted her nephew, Todd Johnson, who worked for the Associated Press. "Why don't you do a story on Rainer?" she said. He talked to his boss then interviewed me a few times, and wrote a story that got picked up by CNN and a number of other major outlets, which was huge. It helped legitimize the streak even more. I'm still amazed that I didn't have to kill, kidnap, or rob anyone to make CNN.

Ginger and I saw each other as often as we could when I was in Colorado — usually she came up to Copper and skied, since I couldn't really take time off to spend in Denver — and one summer she came up to Mt. Hood to visit me.

We talked about getting married … or, to be more precise,

not getting married.

I told her: "You're great, you're funny, you like everything I like. If I were a marrying man, I'd marry you."

"But you're not," she said, still half-questioning me and leaving it open to my reply.

"I'm not," I confirmed. "I don't think I could do that."

Which only confused her. "Well, I don't know what you mean by that."

"A lot of times I'm gone for months. I don't think it would work."

She stopped me there. "Rainer, I think the reason this doesn't bother me is because even if you weren't doing this ski streak, I'm an independent person and so are you. And that's probably why this is working. You need to go off and do your thing. I'm not offended by that."

Her feelings began to change as the streak consumed me more and more later on, especially as I chased 100 million feet and took a leave from my job. But Ginger and I had some great times together. And even though it ended in 2009, I think we both still care about each other.

***

From Colorado to Oregon to Chile, lots of people used to ask me, "Why are you doing this? Do you want to have your name in the book?"

"No," I'd say. "I'm doing it because it hasn't been done before."

I meant that. To do something that no one in your species has done is a unique motivator. You almost feel obligated to push on.

Some of the hardest days to go skiing were the days in Oregon when I knew it was going to be an utter downpour the entire day. I was tempted to quit all the time. Who wouldn't be? Rain beats a skier down, no pun intended. Discipline, however, was never a problem for me — probably because I broke so many wooden spoons with my ass when I misbehaved as a kid. And ironically, sometimes heavy downpours actually helped make the snow better, by smoothing it out and getting rid of the mushy top layer.

It was still never easy to motivate. I'd be lying in my tent in the middle of the forest, listening to it pour outside, all cozy and warm. And I'd know that at some point today, I would have to get up and go spend a bunch of hours outside in this shit. Because I didn't keep my motorcycle at my campsite (to help me not get discovered), I had to walk as far as a mile to the lifts while getting absolutely soaked, just to *start* my ski day.

I learned to be discrete with my campsites. I put the first one closer to Government Camp, the town at the base of Timberline. It was 100 feet back from a road, a 15-minute walk from Govy, and I could get there pretty easily after work. Well, one day some hoodlums threatened a couple of the lifties at Timberline, and they went to find the guys, the mountain manager and everybody. While they were searching, they found my camp. "Rainer," someone said, "this really isn't that great of a spot." I told them I disagreed and thought it was a fine spot. But I didn't go back there the next year.

I put next season's camp a little farther from Govy along a closed road where the truckers' brake-check area is. My bike fit around the rocks that were blocking the road, so I just blazed through and drove up the old road for a while before setting up camp. No one ever spotted that site, and it was really quiet; you'd have an occasional bicycle go by, but that was it. The problem was the mosquitoes. I got chewed alive just going from my bike to my tent late at night. Also, sometimes I'd wake up and smell smoke from the forest fires we had that summer, and wouldn't know whether the fire was getting close to my campsite. So I bailed on that spot after a year, too.

I was always looking for something that gave me easy access to work and living and was out of sight, out of mind. You're not supposed to camp on U.S. Forest Service land for more than 14 days without taking a 14-day break between each stint. But it's not uncommon either, especially around a summer ski resort like Timberline. I kept a low profile — stored all my ski gear at our shop, only had minimal clothing in the tent, never any food or fire rings.

The third spot I picked out was awesome. It was a mile down

from the ski area on an abandoned road, and I camped at a little donut pull-off with a big tree. I could pull in my bike and back up to the tree, and it was invisible from the road. Then I'd walk 100 feet back to my tent. But that was also a campsite where, when the wind was blowing, I'd hear a tree creaking out in the woods and think, where is that tree? That doesn't sound good. It was always on my mind; if I got to my camp early just to change clothes, I'd grab a beer and go wander around, trying to find the tree. But I couldn't find any tree that showed signs of cracking or weakness.

I'm not exaggerating when I say it was a really, really good campsite. It was flat, the mosquitoes weren't bad, and there was no water running through it, so I never got my butt soaked.

The next year I came back to Oregon and went to check out the campsite. The first thing I saw was the creaking tree: It was lying right where my head would've been if I were camping there when it fell. Not an inch in either direction — my head literally would've been smashed by a 3-foot-wide tree. It was freaky, like, all right, time to change venue.

I found a new spot near our shop, where tourists don't really go hiking. It was in a rugged little clump of shrubs and trees, but there was a spot in the middle of the trees for the tent. The sun never hit it, so the tent stayed nice and cool. It was funny because I was so close to the highway but invisible from the highway. And when I parked my snowcat I could walk to my tent in five minutes. So that was sweet.

I used that site for two years, and then I got bolder and moved my tent out to the clearing 100 feet away. The views were incredible; I could see the ski area when I woke up, I could see Mt. Jefferson, and the buzzing bees, crickets at night, and deer roaming around made me feel like I was way out in the wild, even though I was right next to civilization.

As luck would have it, Timberline started trying to promote mountain biking with the use of a lift, and a few Forest Service workers wandered past my tent and found it. They left me a lovely little note: YOU'RE NOT ALLOWED TO CAMP HERE. So I pulled up my stakes, dragged the tent back to the other spot in the trees and never had another problem after that.

The final two years I rented a room down in Govy, ending my camping days. I was 47 years old the last summer I camped at Mt. Hood.

One of the reasons I was able to tolerate living outdoors was because I had my Uncle Adolf and Aunt Gabbi's place to retreat to in Sandy, 45 minutes west of Mt. Hood near Portland. I'd ride my motorcycle down and do my laundry there, sleep in a bed, load all my logs and ski data from the week, and catch up with two of my favorite people. My streak didn't help a lot of the relationships in my life, but it certainly brought me closer to Adolf and Gabbi.

Adolf is my dad's brother. He came to the U.S. in 1953, right after he graduated high school in Germany (he grew up in Bavaria, in a town north of Munich). He joined the Army and served for two years, which, if you think about it — joining the U.S. military as a German man only eight years after World War 2 — seemingly would make him a target. But he said he never had any problems, even as a 19-year-old plebe. It was the height of the Cold War and the Korean War was just winding down, so Uncle Sam needed everybody he could get, Uncle Adolf included.

After the Army, Adolf got a degree in forestry from the University of Michigan and worked seven years for the U.S. Forest Service. His last assignment was to supervise the contract the Forest Service had with the company that ran Timberline Lodge (the Forest Service owned it, but contracted someone else to run it). He started a lumber company when he got out of the Forest Service and has been doing that ever since.

He's 82 now, and Gabbi is 80. But you'd never know it — he's trim and fit, and she's a bundle of energy who still cooks delicious meals and speaks German, English, Japanese, and enough Russian to get by. They met in grade school in Germany and have been in love for most of their lives. After settling in Oregon, they found a gorgeous 20-acre property in Sandy and built their house using a combination of Douglas fir, Hemlock fir, and cedar from their lumberyard. Whenever I went to visit them, I'd sit with Adolf on their deck and sip my Crown while he drank his scotch, and I'd tell him the latest stories from my streak. He was always interested, which I appreciated.

Adolf jokes that in an area where he was quite well known, his identity switched to "Rainer's uncle" once I started spending summers at Timberline. He's being modest. In fact, his biggest effect on my streak was something he said every now and again that stuck with me. I'd ride down to Sandy kind of worn out from a week of rain or having to deal with broken lifts, and he could tell that I was not exactly thrilled to continue my streak. Because after five years, I did have some weird thoughts run through my mind, like: What am I doing? I could just bag this at any time, and it'll be a world record. But Adolf would set me straight with one sentence.

"You're not a quitter, are ya?"

It was all I needed to hear. From then on, a little voice in my head would repeat that whenever I was feeling down. "You're not a quitter, are ya?" My thinking would immediately change to: Shut up, Rainer! Stop your whining and get out there and do it. I've never had sympathy for crybabies anyway.

***

The winter of 2007-08 was a deep one in northern Colorado. The storms just kept pulsing through Summit County, one after the other. It was a great season to be a powder skier. It was also a leap year, which meant I had to ski an extra day to finish five years.

Because we got a lot of snow, we also got a lot of wind and frigid days. I got sick of it after a while, but I always made myself stay out long enough to hit my numbers. It was like going to work at my vertical office — that's how I looked at it.

Crowded days were always tougher to maximize my skiing. I had to ski the human slalom course, and the lift lines get long when the snow's good. I was — and will be for the rest of my life — a huge proponent of the singles line. Skiing is all about efficiency. I live in a ski-in, ski-out condo; I can ski across my parking lot to the lift. It makes a huge difference when you fill every seat on every chair. If I saw three people on a quad chair ahead of me, I didn't hesitate to say,

"Add one." If I'm the next guy in line and there's a spot on a chair, I'm taking it, I don't care who you are. It took me quite a few years of working at Copper to convey that concept to lift operations and mountain management.

I was also allowed to use the employee line, which was an advantage. But there were times when the singles line was faster than the employee line. I'd scope it out from a half-mile up the hill, because visually you're able to. And I'd make a decision right there. If the lift was stopped, then I'd scream down to the Magic Mile for another thousand feet of vertical without standing around thinking about it. My approach was to get maximum vert any way I could. That meant I was always on the lookout for rookie button pushers working the lifts, or trigger-happy veterans. You don't want to be on a lift that stops all the time if you're trying to go fast.

The highlight of Year 5 took place in Chile during the fall of 2008. I was racking up vert at Valle Nevado, trying to build my Slush Fund, and I went out for some cocktails one night to celebrate a great day of skiing. I met two guys in their mid-30s from Los Angeles who built satellite transmission components for TV stations — and made a lot of money doing it. We were sitting at different tables chatting about the snow when three knockout Brazilian girls walked in. They sat at the booth behind my friends from L.A., so the guys couldn't look at them.

I had a perfect view of the girls from where I was sitting, so the guys asked if they could join me at my table and chat up these girls, buy them some wine, and get something going. The guys tried to get us all laid, but the girls weren't really into it. We found out later that they were models for some kind of South American beauty product. At any rate, one of the L.A. boys asked me what I was doing down there and I told him about my streak. "Shit!" he yelled. "I read about you!" He looked at his buddy then back at me. "We've always wanted to go heli snowboarding, and we're renting a chopper tomorrow. We've got two open seats and we're paying for the whole thing. Do you want to go?"

I think my mouth said, "Yes" before my brain instructed it to.

The next day, after skiing about 30,000 feet in the morning, the helicopter picked us up at Valle Nevado and took us into some of the surrounding peaks near the Argentina border. We skied down a dormant volcano where the glacier had receded enough to expose a major cliff, so you had to avoid that. We skied dry powder at the top then slush by the time we got down to the chopper, 5,000 feet below. After three long runs, my friends said, "OK, that's enough fun, let's go home." The helicopter company was charging by the minute and each guy paid $1,000 for our three runs. I tipped the guide $200 because I got to ski for free and because I knew him — he'd picked me up when I was hitchhike-skiing after the ski area closed the year before.

    The chopper dropped us off inside the ski area, so I skied down to the base and continued riding lifts for another two hours. By the time the day was over, I'd skied more than 50,000 feet.

IX

Even though I was fully committed to skiing every day — for a significant amount of time, if possible — I also got wistful. I was missing out on a lot of life. When summer hit Colorado, all my friends stopped skiing and did other stuff. They went on vacations, sailed, surfed, lay on the beach, and soaked up the sun. I did none of that. I just thought about it.

In early 2009, I met up with my old friend Rude and learned the rumors about him were true: He was moving to Iowa and leaving the ski industry. I was sad to hear it; I always am when I learn a fellow ski bum has had enough of our life. It instinctively makes me question my own subscription to ski-bum living, for a few minutes at least.

So did a lot of things. Like working on holidays, for instance, or missing family reunions, birthday parties, and funerals. I worked on Christmas a lot, simply because the date fell on a day I was scheduled to work. It would have been nice to be with my family that day, and I know my mom and siblings didn't always love that I missed the get-togethers, but if I had to work I also got to ski, and skiing on Christmas wasn't all bad.

Some of my best ski buddies were often out skiing on Christmas; every now and then members of my family would come up to ski. Skiing is pretty spiritual to me, the freedom you have, and this was always reinforced on Christmas. There's almost never a crowd because everyone's celebrating the holiday. It's sort of like New Year's Day — no one's skiing because they're all too hungover. And because Christmas comes during one of the coldest stretches of the year, usually the snow is good too.

Unfortunately the holidays are just as prone to life's perils. Shortly after Christmas 2008, on December 30, tragedy struck our tight-knit crew at Copper. An old friend named Brian Mahon, whom I had trained to make snow at Copper back in the day, was working as general manager of Eldora Mountain Resort outside Boulder. He went to work that day same as any, but a rogue liftie who had only worked at the resort for a month took Brian's life in a senseless and cowardly act of rage.

The liftie, Derik Bonestroo, came to work disgruntled, dressed in black, and carrying a semiautomatic pistol. He apparently wasn't the best employee from what I heard. Right before the 7 a.m. meeting where everyone talks about the upcoming day, he walked into the locker room and fired a shot into the ceiling to get people's attention. Then he started spewing some gibberish about converting people to Christianity. Brian heard the shot from outside the locker room and went to investigate. The moment he walked in, the liftie shot him in the chest and head, killing him instantly.

The killer then fled Eldora in his car. A sheriff's deputy passed him going the opposite direction on Colorado 119 as he raced to the shooting site. The deputy spun around and went after Bonestroo, who pulled over and started firing at the deputy after a two-mile chase. He blasted the deputy's SUV with a hail of bullets, shooting out its windows and tires, but the deputy was able to grab his high-powered assault rifle and shoot back. He shot the guy dead during their gunfight, which I was happy to hear.

The way I look at it is this: It was devastating that Brian lost his life and it still is, but he probably saved 10 to 20 other people's lives by taking the bullet and freaking the kid out, so that he ran away instead of staying there and killing however many people he wanted to kill (they found later that he'd killed his cat in his cabin in Nederland and believe he was on a mission to do a lot more harm than he did). I was also glad that the deputy shot the kid dead so we're not paying taxes to keep some dumb little criminal alive in jail, feeding him and clothing him. I'm glad the rules of the Old West took over and that he's gone too, as harsh as that sounds.

Brian's death affected me deeply. We get pretty close to each other when we work together, moving equipment around at 12,000 feet on dark, frigid nights. Copper has always been like that — you rely on the guy next to you, and he relies on you. I put in a lot of time training Brian, so we were tight. He respected the work I did and gave me a long leash to be myself so long as the work got done. I've never wanted to be a boss, which made it awesome to have a guy above me who trusted me. My boss Brad was shaken up for weeks because Brian and he lived together for years and were really close. More than anything, we hated to lose a friend who was so happy all the time. Life needs more of those guys and fewer psychopaths.

***

Grooming snow can seem like a tedious way to make a living, and it is to an extent, but it's misunderstood overall. An uninitiated bystander may think the operator isn't doing anything but sitting in front of a window watching the world crawl by in super slow motion. On the contrary, grooming snow is hands on, minds on all the time. It's very rare that you can just let the cat go and it grooms snow the way it's supposed to be done. When people groom that way, it's apparent to me when I look at the trail.

Back when I started grooming at Copper, there were only four of us and the cats weren't nearly as sophisticated as they are now. I learned in a DMC 3700; it basically had a straight push blade with wings on the side. You couldn't see the blade, all you could see were the corners. So it was basically grooming by feel, then looking at what you left behind to see if you did it right. Whereas now, with the new cats, you're staring at the blade and can see everything as it happens.

It takes a deft touch to prep the trails so they're perfect for all the discerning intermediate skiers the next morning. The trails that we let the rookies groom have snowmaking on them for a smooth base, and they've been dozed out to be no-brainers. The operators are just putting the surface texture on the trails, instead of doing repair work, taking the high spots out, or rebuilding the trail so it's consistently the same depth.

Each day there's a new challenge, especially once the snow starts melting. Where's the new rock? Or the new stump? You have to pay attention because if you nail one of those rocks at full-tilt boogie, you're going to destroy the cat, which is not an inexpensive problem. A $250,000 cat is a pretty cheap cat. If you want a winch or a Zaugg pipe cutter, you're looking at more like $375,000. One time an operator in Oregon nailed a stump so hard that his head snapped forward and broke the windshield, which cost $2,400 to replace. He called me down to check his pupils, but he was OK. To break a window as high-tech as the ones in our cats takes a solid force. I actually know other guys who have knocked themselves unconscious when they hit something in their cat.

I've never knocked myself out, but I've tagged rocks hard enough that it bent the hydraulic rams on the blade. That's an expensive fix too. But I don't know what's underneath the snow on every square inch of the 100 acres I groom each night.

Grooming is only part of my heavy-machinery devotion. I got interested in machines back when I was a teenager working at the GoKart track in Estes; that's where I learned how to take things apart and rebuild them. In addition to grooming at Copper, I also drove huge dirt movers in the summer or just skipped the summer entirely and went to the Southern Hemisphere to work on their snow.

Grooming and snowmaking have taken me around the world, from Oregon to Asia. One of the most memorable trips happened in the winter of 1990-91 when I went to work at Muju Resort in South Korea, which was (and still may be) the world's biggest ski area to be started and completed within a year's time. A friend whom I'd taught how to groom landed a job at Muju for a lot of money, and he chose me to teach them how to make snow.

The Koreans couldn't really pronounce my name, and even though I had a translator shadowing me for most of my time there, the guys I was working with started calling me Rhino instead — actually "Rhino No. 1," since that's how they talk there. They'd shout it, almost like a cheer: "Rhino No. 1!" I didn't mind at all. My old buddy Duck from Estes Park gave me that nickname — Rhino — when we were kids. It was cool to have it be my name again on the other side of the world.

My translator basically went everywhere I went, because I had no way to communicate with anyone. He ended up being the best snowmaker they had because he watched everything I did. Making snow is fickle work, and hard; you're not just freezing water and spraying it out a hose, you're dragging hoses and metal equipment around a bony mountain, over dirt, rocks, and weeds. Snowmakers have four-wheelers to help them now, but 30 years ago, we walked everywhere we went. It was brutal on the body.

I could always tell what kind of snow a gun was making by the noise coming out of it. At Muju I would start 40 guns and get them all running, let the system stabilize, then go back and check them to be sure the snow was the right consistency. Once the temperature dropped down to the nightly low, it really wouldn't change the rest of the night, so I just let the guns go, jumped in a cat, and helped out the groomers until 4 or 5 in the morning. Then I'd shut down all the guns, get something to eat, and go to sleep.

For being built in a year, Muju was astounding. We had two high-speed quads, two other quad lifts, two double chairs, and two Poma lifts. There was stadium lighting for night skiing and all the towers had surround sound. You felt like you were at a party on a giant football field.

Muju, which is located five hours from Seoul, also built an escalator from the rental shop up to the trails, so people wearing ski boots for the first time would ride the escalator to go skiing. When someone fell on their way up, it took out a lot of other people and sent them tumbling down the escalator, which was hilarious.

One of my wackiest adventures took place on my way home from the Muju gig. I decided to stop and visit a bunch of places before I returned to the U.S., starting in Taiwan (I wish I'd spent a week there, but I was sick of rice and Asia) then moving on to Singapore and Australia before finishing in New Zealand. I had met some people in Fiji who lived in Australia, so they picked me up at the airport in Elbert and gave me a map with a list of places to check out. I bought a bus pass to go up the east coast of Australia and pretty much stopped in any town the bus stopped in.

Along the way, I decided I'd learn to SCUBA dive. I caught a ferry out to a backpacker's hostel on Magnetic Island, near Townsville, and met a guy who was offering advanced certification dives. I had also heard about the Yongala shipwreck, which at the time was rated the No. 6 shipwreck dive in the world. So after doing a handful of shallower dives, I booked the Yongala as my deep dive, because you have to do a 100-foot dive to get advanced certification.

The weather turned sour and windy on the day we were scheduled to dive the Yongala, and most boats canceled their trips (on a nice day you'll find three or four boats there). My boat, however, said it was still going. It was a 55-foot craft named, ironically, Pure Pleasure.

That day was the captain's first time piloting her own tour. Another captain was onboard just in case, but once we got to the wreck, he and the dive master were focused on setting the ascent/descent line to the Yongala, a crucial component due to the six-foot swells on the ocean that day.

The captain decided to try and position the boat right above the ascent/descent line to make it easier for us to just plop into the ocean where we needed to be. But in doing so, she turned the boat around and started to back into the whitecaps. We were all putting on our dive gear and fins, standing on the back of the boat ready to jump in. A couple of people wondered aloud, "Why is she backing into the waves?" Then a few swells broke over the back of the boat, sending thousands of gallons of water into the cockpit. Almost immediately, the boat started to sink. As more waves broke over the stern, it got worse and worse. People started to panic, because it was obvious the bilge pumps that flush the boat couldn't keep up with the amount of water coming in.

Everybody started to abandon the ship, freaking out as they dove overboard 50 miles out to sea. I went into the boat's galley and made sure everybody was out, because I had my full tank on and could breathe underwater. By the time everyone was in the sea, the back door was halfway underwater and going down quickly. So I ended up bailing out of a side window; my tank hit the window and I had to do a weird twisting maneuver to get out. I didn't have fins, but I scavenged two fins that were floating and put them on.

I grabbed the three girls in our group and dragged them to the life raft; by that time most everyone else was already there. We had two life rafts tied together so we'd make a bigger target in the ocean for the rescue helicopters that were already on their way. We also had a small dinghy with a motor tethered to us. People started to get seasick, but in an underrated move of brilliance, they all sat in one life raft and we sat in the other one (seasickness is kind of contagious).

Despite the initial terror, it was actually kind of cool, almost like a whitewater raft trip in the ocean. The helicopters showed up not long after we all got into the rafts. The first one was the Queensland rescue chopper. They started taking passengers out of the seasick raft, and once they were all gone, it flew away and a military Blackhawk chopper arrived and lifted the rest of us out. They could lift two of us at a time, so the dive master and I got rescued together. A news chopper had followed the call for help and took a photograph of us dangling between the raft and the chopper. Which, of course, is what I sent to my mom: us on the cover of the next day's newspaper, along with a note that read, "Hey Mom, having a great time. Miss you!" She got a chuckle out of it.

As the saga continued, we got dropped off at the helipad at the airport, and they took us to the police station. I was one of the last people to give a statement. I told the cops, "I need to get to the ferry to get back out to the island where my ID and money are." I hadn't eaten all day. I was starving, still in a wetsuit, no shoes, nothing. After I gave my statement about what happened, they dropped me off at the wrong ferry dock. I saw two guys swabbing the decks on an idle boat and said, "You guys are done for the day, right?" Their eyes lit up. "Aw, shit, mate, we just saw you on the tele!"

It turned out that my brief television interview had been sent to the Australian Broadcasting Corporation and already aired on the news.

"What was it like out there?" the reporter asked me.

"Wet," I said.

"Anything else you want to say?"

"Yeah: I'd like to have a beer now."

The anchor on the news was laughing his ass off during my interview. "This is what an American tourist said!"

Anyway, the deck-swabbing guys got on the radio and called the correct ferry, which was the last one going to Magnetic Island. They were just departing but they swung over and grabbed me; I jumped from one boat to another at trolling speed. We made it back, partied a bit, and crashed.

I actually did get to go out and dive the Yongala, but we took a much bigger boat, a marine research vessel that was 90 feet long. It only went 8 mph, so we left at midnight on a full moon with the ocean as calm as it gets, like a big glassy lake. Instead of sleeping in my berth, I said, "Hey, do you mind if I just sleep up on the deck?" They didn't mind at all, so I basically camped out on the Great Barrier Reef.

We reached the dive site at 6 a.m., had breakfast, then plunged down to the shipwreck. The dive was as extraordinary as advertised. I actually had a 6-foot-wide bull ray come out of the Yongala's cargo holds and take a look at me. I was banging my knife on the tank to alert people. I'd never seen so many wild animals and organisms in such a colorful environment. It was the best day of my life.

***

I've always been in tune with our natural world and comfortable in weird situations, which often go hand in hand. One time I ate freshly caught ahi tuna 20 miles off the coast of Hawaii in a 45-foot sailboat while chasing a hole in the clouds to see the solar eclipse. I've skied on steamy volcanoes and obviously spent plenty of time in avalanche terrain. Still, I have a strange fear of lightning.

I know the chances are low, but when you're up high and the

air turns electric, it feels like you're about to get hit every time. And there's no way to know when you actually are the target (in fact, despite the 700,000-to-1 odds of getting struck, 240,000 people are struck every year worldwide). That's why whenever there was lightning in the area while I was skiing, I got the hell out of there. It didn't matter how much I'd skied that day; it was enough.

I've been caught in lightning storms so many times on snow — late spring in Colorado, midsummer in Oregon, and late spring in South America — that I've noticed a weird phenomenon right before the lightning starts to hit where I'm skiing. The snow turns a really strange color, almost a greenish turquoise. Every time I see that color, it's a good indication that lightning is coming. Doesn't matter if I'm in the northern hemisphere or the southern. I've never seen the same color on the snow without lightning nearby.

I still haven't been struck by lightning, thankfully. But I did come across a massive landslide one time in Chile right after it swept across the road I was driving on. It was late in Year 6, September 9, 2009. I was weary from my midnight run in Oregon, things with Ginger were unraveling, and as usual, I was stressed about all the logistics I was facing to keep the streak alive. I flew into Santiago from Portland, rented a car, grabbed a burger at McDonald's, and headed up the road to Valle Nevado to ski.

A short way up the mountain I saw what had to be 100 policemen and firemen and a bunch of heavy equipment sifting through the mud, searching. It was obvious that something had washed across the road: three houses were utterly demolished, with truck-size boulders lying around the scene. I've seen enough floods that I know what a flood looks like. This wasn't a flood. It was a landslide. It had happened during the night, and everyone was searching for a missing mother and child.

I had just picked up a local hitchhiker and had a bunch of cars following me. We passed through two more mudslides as responders flagged us through each disaster zone. After we were through the wreckage, I pulled over to let all the other cars go by then pulled back onto the road. A young *carabinero,* or local cop, pulled me over right before I turned up to Valle Nevado and asked to check my papers —

probably because he wasn't used to seeing polite drivers in a place where all the locals race each other up the mountain. He was also young and was trying to impress the older cops.

It turned out the car's registration was expired. After some tough negotiations through my Chilean hitchhiker, who spoke decent English, the cop took my license but let us go with a ticket for the expired registration. (If I was passing into Argentina on one of my trips, I checked every document I had to make sure it was current; but since I was staying in Chile this time, I didn't look at everything too closely, which turned out to be stupid).

I finally made it to El Colorado that afternoon and took a few runs before calling it a day. I was beat by then. I called the rental car company the next morning and they promised to send someone up to fix everything on Monday. The guy never showed. They promised the same thing for the following Monday. Another no-show. Two guys finally came the third time and brought another car, but at that point, I told them to take both cars back because I still didn't have a license and I didn't want to go to jail for driving without one.

I skied with a purpose that trip — when I got there, I was 11 days behind my million-feet-per-month pace; when I left, I was 17 days ahead. The date when I was scheduled to fly home to Colorado approached, and I still didn't have my license back. I skied over to a small resort named Farellones that had a police station at its base. I explained what happened, the cops took my name, and luckily a guy I knew through our mutual affinity for motorcycles, Pedro, was working on one of the cops' cars outside. He talked to the cops and, as I understood, they gave him directions to the police station where my license was being held. "Rainer," Pedro said, "I'll get your license back. I'll find you when I do."

Satisfied for the day, I left to start hitchhiking back to Valle Nevado. After three hours of standing on the side of the road, a brand-new Mercedes stopped and picked me up. Two old-timers from La Parva were inside. Luckily one guy spoke German so I could talk to him. He told me the guy driving the Mercedes was the first Chilean ever to ski in the Olympics and had free Mercedes for life. They were really interesting guys; getting to talk to them was well worth the three-hour wait on the side of the road.

I still hadn't heard from Pedro after a few days, so I called another friend named John Hussey who knew Pedro too. John is a ski instructor at Beaver Creek during Colorado's winter, then he heads down and teaches at La Parva during our summer. He's also a ski racer and had been following my streak, so I asked if he could call Pedro and get my license back. He talked to Pedro then called me back and said, "Call me when you're leaving for the airport and I'll meet you at the intersection and give you your license back."

As bizarre as it was, the Canadian ski team was giving me a ride down to Santiago because I didn't have a rental car. We met up with John on the way to the airport, he handed me my license, and I gave him 20,000 pesos to give to Pedro as a thank-you gift, as well as a signed picture of me and my motorcycle with my kayak, fly rod, and skis on the bike.

Pedro was always grateful for that gesture when I saw him in subsequent years. I believe stuff like that goes a long way, especially in foreign countries (I also brought Heinekens to the lifties at Nevados de Chillan). Not counting the cops, the Chilean people — most notably my friend Claudio Diaz, whose kids Chopo and Soledad are among the hottest skiers in the country — always treated me kindly and gave me extra incentive to keep my streak going another year, so I could go back down and see them again.

And it wasn't just them I looked forward to seeing down there. Because I constantly needed snow, I was on the same schedule and a similar world tour as the U.S. Ski Team. I became friends with a lot of them in Oregon, just from riding chairlifts together. They were there to train, I was there to ski bum, and every day those two worlds merge on the hill.

I got to know World Cup moguls champion Pat Deneen particularly well, as well as a bunch of the racers (Bode Miller even complimented my skiing commitment while talking to a mutual friend of ours). During that same 2009 trip to Chile, I bumped into Sarah Schleper, a Vail product who was, at the time, one of the top-ranked slalom skiers in the world.

I had seen Sarah that summer before we both left for South

America. It was shortly after a messy episode unfolded with some punk kids and their dad at Timberline. One of our mechanics at the time would bring his kids to work and leave them in the shop while he went out to work on cats. The kids got restless one day, so a mechanic suggested they go search for treasure under the lift.

My tent happened to be under the lift in the trees, and I was just waking up after working until 3 in the morning. It was 10 o'clock when I heard laughing and giggling outside my tent. Then all of a sudden, the kids started saying things like, "Let's throw a rock at it and see if there's anyone in there!" So I sat up, luckily, and was about to unzip the tent and see what's going on when a rock came through the tent and landed on my pillow, right where my head would've been. It was as big as a softball with really sharp edges; it would've probably cut me up if not knocked me out.

Enraged, I chased the kids down, walked them up to the shop, and made them take a piece of paper out and write down their parents' names and phone numbers so I could call Mommy and Daddy and tell them what happened. I realized their dad was our cat mechanic, so I gave him a piece of my mind when I saw him that afternoon. He and I got into it because he didn't really do anything to punish the kids except not let them snowboard. I liked the guy for a long time, but after that happened we were no longer friends.

At any rate, I had told Sarah Schleper about that incident when I saw her at Mt. Hood. A month later, when I saw her again in Chile, she asked me about my "tent situation" and whether I'd gotten a new tent to replace the one with the hole in it. Sarah stuck out because she always had whiskers drawn on her face and you'd see her carrying the gates, tearing down courses, slipping the ruts, doing whatever she could to help out her coaches. Very few elite racers worked as hard as she did.

I told her I was waiting until I got back to Colorado to get a new tent, but that I appreciated her asking about it.

"No problem," she said. "Keep the dream alive."

As a middle-aged ski bum, to hear that from an Olympian gave me a deep sense of satisfaction.

"I will," I told Sarah.

X

Everyone has a different view of what characterizes a ski bum. Literally defined, you could say we are bums who ski. But I don't really agree with that, because some people think of bums as being lazy or worthless. And we're not. We're just motivated by different things than most of society. For that reason I think we belong in our own classification. If you went searching for the nucleus of skiing, you would find a bunch of ski bums: people who live primarily to ski and fit everything else in their life around that pursuit.

How can you recognize a ski bum? You see them on the lift or in the lift lines a lot, sometimes wearing shoddy gear, but not always. You see them hanging around town, nursing a beer and a shot in the 5 o'clock après hour at the end of the bar. For ski bums, work is a means to go skiing, nothing more. No matter what they do for money, they make sure they're working during the hours they can't be skiing. Or they allow time in the day to ski for three or four hours, and then go to work, or vice versa. They're not so worried about status and how they look and smell. They're more concerned with getting on the snow and having equipment that performs well day in and day out.

And they're characters. They add color to a winter world that can often seem black and white and gray for months at a time. Ski bums tend to smile a lot. And laugh. This is because ski bums are generally happy. That's kind of the whole point of ski bumming: it satisfies your soul.

I suppose the first ski bums I met were in Estes Park. As kids we didn't realize we were destined for such an existence; we just loved to ski and hang out at Hidden Valley together. But looking back, the men we admired — and aspired to be like — were classic ski bums. Greg Hurt, my old race coach, personified the term. When he told me he thought I had World Cup potential, it was like hearing Vince Lombardi tell you he thought you'd make a good linebacker.

A bunch of the guys I hung out with in high school formed a group called the Allenspark Tree Team, or AP Tree Team for short. They were basically old-school Estes gangsters, in the ski-bum sense of that word. They would skin up and ski backcountry lines around Rocky Mountain National Park, or use their old, ramshackle snowmobiles to skip the uphill slog. They bushwhacked up and down pretty much every skiable run between Nederland and Hidden Valley.

I had a Tree Team T-shirt and was loosely affiliated with the group, but I didn't ski with them much. A lot of us worked at Hidden Valley together or hung out at Lonigans or the Wheel Bar. My buddy KZ was a big part of the AP Tree Team, as was a guy I came to know later named Pinecone. Pinecone's real name is Dave Pines. We met sometime in the '80s, but neither of us can remember exactly when or where.

Everyone comes to skiing on their own terms, but of all my ski-bum friends, Pinecone was the latest bloomer. He grew up in Pennsylvania, the son of a chemist, and moved to Colorado when he was 19. He settled in Nederland, an old hippie community outside of Boulder with a strong collection of mountain athletes, but didn't start skiing for another 11 years. Early on he was a snowshoer and cross-country skier. Luckily one of his snowshoe friends also liked to ski, and every time they stopped to take a break during one of their walks in the woods, the guy would look at Pinecone and say, "Well, now's a good time to extoll upon you the virtues of skiing." He wouldn't let up. One night he and Pinecone snowshoed for 10 hours under the full moon. They were dead tired when they finished. As Pinecone tells it, "I saw the guy a few days later, and he got right in my face, eye to eye, less than a foot away. He was like, '*WHEN* are you going to put skis on?' And I surprised myself as much as him by saying, 'Let's go.'"

From that day forward, Pinecone's winter life has revolved around skiing. "Gravity kind of caught me" is how he puts it. He skied at Lake Eldora with a bunch of the AP Tree Team guys before graduating to A-Basin. He's a telemarker like I am and skis 100 days a year. You can always recognize him at the Basin because he has a thick beard and big mop of curly hair that spills out from under his winter hat. And he's always smiling in the lift line.

Like a lot of ski bums, Pinecone does what he must to get by. He works Sunday mornings at the co-op in Nederland to get a deal on groceries, he's a part-time bike mechanic, and he turns wood with his lathe, crafting bowls and spoons or repairing table legs. "I have a lot of old skills," he says.

Pinecone and I have skied some memorable runs down Sundance in Rocky Mountain National Park — including one with KZ when we saw a wild wolf walking down the road after we skied — but I mainly see him at A-Basin now. One year he was one of the locals whom the Basin — which is known locally as The Legend — featured on its trail map. People would walk up to Pinecone and say, "Are you the Legend?" And he'd reply, "No, the mountain is the Legend. We're just the characters."

Still, Pinecone never took skiing too seriously. When I bumped into him during my vertical assaults, he'd convince me to join him for a run down the steeps of Pallavicini. I'd say, "You better not get me hurt," and Pinecone would chuckle. As he likes to say, "Skiing's not a matter of life and death. It's way more important than that."

Another member of the AP Tree Team, Bob Sequeira, was nicknamed Squank. We used to make snow together at Hidden Valley. My best memory of Squank took place at a cabin where he used to live in Meeker Park, on the east side of Longs Peak. Squank and I were sitting on the roof drinking beer and bagging rays when we heard a hell of a ruckus down below. We went down and checked it out, and to our astonishment, we found two hogs that had dumped his garbage in the kitchen and were tearing through it like bears fresh off hibernation. We chased them out of the house and grabbed some firewood on our way through the yard. As we ran after them down the road, trying to scare them enough that they'd never come back, I threw a piece of firewood at the pigs. It nailed Squank in the middle of his back. I felt horrible, but it was funny as hell. We laughed for the rest of the afternoon about the entire episode, sitting on the roof drinking our beers.

Back in those days, everyone had a nickname. When I worked at the GoKart track, my buddies were Arms, Nozy, and Toad. They called me Ernie, for reasons I can't recall. Another friend was known as Moby, because he was huge like the whale. Then there was Wolf, who could pick up chicks like no one else. In his honor, we gave out "Wolf tickets" to pretty girls we met in town, so they'd come down to the track and see us in our element, all studly and tan and eligible. At Copper, we had Sugar Bear, Rude, and Space, a.k.a. Don Coleman, who often walked into a room with a faraway look on his face, like he was stuck in a different galaxy.

It should come as no surprise that two of the most devoted ski bums I've ever met also had nicknames. One was CJ ("Crazy John") Mueller, a former "speed skier" who set a few world records for going faster than anyone ever had on skis (his mark of 136 mph gained the most renown, even if it was broken a few hours later). He grew up in Denver the son of an aerospace engineer but adopted Breckenridge as his hometown once he dropped out of college at the Colorado School of Mines. CJ earned his nickname from the stunts he pulled on snow at Breck. He used to rocket around the mountain every day and sail more than 200 feet off jumps he and his friends built on Peak 8. He was also the founder of the Ridge Street Rowdies, a faux motorcycle gang that gave Breck some of its color in the '70s and '80s.

When his alpine racing career fizzled, CJ took up speed skiing, which, as a 1989 profile of him in *People Magazine* explained, essentially involved tucking his knees into his armpits and straightlining down 45-degree slopes on downhill boards. I spent a lot of time working with CJ for Stan Miller Excavating, running heavy equipment and stacking rock walls at construction sites with my old buddy Boo. I still see CJ out skiing, mostly in the spring at A-

Basin, where everyone recognizes me for my flat-brim floppy hat and Hawaiian shirt.

CJ had some problems with his hips in later years, but he still skis 150 days a season and is often the first guy in line on a powder day. He once compared my streak to Cal Ripken's 17-year record of 2,632 consecutive games played. "Cal Ripken didn't play baseball every day. But Rainer went out and did it every day," CJ said. "He didn't have an offseason to recover."

As for his own devotion to skiing, CJ says, "I just do it because I love the snow and I love being in the mountains. That's something that can be really powerful."

CJ was buddies with another classic ski bum I came to befriend through the years, "T-Bar Tommy" Larkin, who survived one of the most remarkable stories I've ever heard.

Tommy moved to Colorado from Pennsylvania in 1974 and took a job patrolling at A-Basin for $2.75 an hour. He hated having to work while he was skiing, so he quit after a year and started tuning skis at night. Eventually he moved to Breckenridge and became something of a local legend for his commitment to the ski-bum life. When all his oldest friends started getting married and having kids and taking on mortgages, Tommy, an only child, never did any of that.

He lived in the same one-bedroom apartment for nearly 30 years. When you walked in, you first noticed the ski-tuning bench set up on his breakfast bar, then the 30 pairs of skis mounted chronologically on his wall, then his one-piece ski suits hanging in the corner. In his late 50s, when his friends' ski days threatened to dip below 100, he skied three straight years of more than 200 days. CJ described Tommy this way: "He's the king of the ski bums. He doesn't rip, but nobody loves skiing more than he does."

On December 13, 2006, Tommy went skiing at Breckenridge same as always. After a couple of hours he headed home, same route as always. While skiing down a green run called Sawmill, at 1:36 p.m., he suffered a massive cardiac arrest and, for all intents and purposes, dropped dead. An anesthesiologist vacationing from Louisiana happened to be skiing a few feet behind Tommy when he collapsed, and immediately stopped to assist. Tommy had no pulse and was not breathing. The anesthesiologist started administering CPR. Tommy vomited into the man's mouth, but the doc continued.

Soon ski patrol arrived and took over the chest compressions. On a whim, one of the responding patrollers had grabbed an external defibrillator while running out the door. They put it on Tommy's chest and shocked his heart, hoping it was still beating at one of the two rhythms out of a dozen that are shockable. Then they sent a tube down his throat into his lungs. Another shock. More compressions. Finally, they checked for a pulse.

"He's got a pulse!" someone shouted.

Tommy was flown by helicopter to a hospital in Denver, where he lay in bed for a week. He doesn't remember going skiing the day his heart stopped or anything from the following five days. When he got home, an interesting thing happened. People he barely knew came up to him and told him he was special to them, that the interactions they've had have meant something to them. "The things they've said to me, they're things you might only hear at a funeral," Tommy said at the time. It struck me as an example of the strange but true role that ski bums play in a ski town. They're the binding force. Without ski bums, a ski town has no soul.

Tommy, like CJ, like me, like all of us, feels an innate connection to not only snow but the lifestyle. Skiing is kind of like his mental spine. "It gives you that grasp, you know? Not even skiing the whole day, but just to get out there for two hours," he says. "It grounds you."

In the wake of his accident, the local newspaper ran a story about Tommy's survival. He talked about a friend who had collapsed and died while skiing just a few months before his incident. He still has no idea why he lived and his friend died, but he did offer a classic long-shot theory. "Maybe I've done enough skiing that the ski gods weren't gonna let me go out on a green run," he said.

Whenever I bumped into Tommy at A-Basin, we'd take a few runs together. We had a lot of mutual respect for each other as ski bums, I think. When a local magazine interviewed him about my streak in early 2012, he said, "It's beyond the realm of normal comprehension. It's so hard to ski 50 days in a row, or 100 days in a row. But 2,993 days in a row? My god. To change countries and hemispheres and never miss a day, that's almost a military move. It takes so much precision."

One day in June, Tommy and I were riding the Black Mountain Express together at A-Basin. We took a guy from the singles line and quickly learned that he thought he was a big deal. He was bragging about the number of days and vertical he had skied that season, quite a lot if I recall. But we weren't having any of it. "That's a good start," I told him. Tommy laughed and said he was up to however many days — more than our new friend, at any rate — then asked about my numbers. I told them I'd skied 2,772 days in a row and 90.8 million vertical feet. Later on, Tommy told me that he laughed about that lift ride all day.

None of this is to say that ski bumming isn't without its hardships or consequences. This got reinforced to all of us in November 2009 when a vintage ski bum named Charlie Toups was thrown in jail for camping on public land close to the slopes. Charlie was well known in Colorado ski country; he always wore the same brown jacket and looked like a sack of potatoes. The Denver Post covered his ordeal pretty heavily and chronicled his life as a ski bum, from California to Oregon to Utah to Colorado. Charlie claimed to have skied at least 120 days every winter since the 1970s. He slept in an old pickup with a shoddy camper on the back, and before that, he slept in a Volkswagen Beetle. When he failed to pay a ticket for overstaying his allotted time on public land, a Forest Service officer confronted him at A-Basin and found some pot and a pipe in his jacket pocket.

He spent 61 days in jail before admitting he was originally in the wrong, which got him released in mid-January. "It's a shame this resolution wasn't reached the day he was arrested, so he didn't spend half the ski season in jail," his public defender said. But the winter of 2009-'10 started out so dry, we just assumed Charlie stayed in jail until it started snowing enough to make the skiing good again.

***

Ski bumming affects every aspect of your life, relationships included. By 2009, Ginger and I were on the rocks. For a long time she accepted the way I prioritized my streak, but eventually something changed. We would hang out together, same as ever, and she'd say things like, "I feel alone when I'm with you." She believed the streak had become too controlling, that it left no room for anything — or anyone — else. In a sense she was right: I wasn't going to let anything or anyone get in the way of my daily skiing. But what she didn't understand — what nobody could fully understand — was that my streak *required* me to think like that. Especially in the later years, when the record had grown to more than 2,500 days, I couldn't afford to let my guard down, no matter how much other people wanted me to.

Toward the end of our seven years together, Ginger used to joke with me. "Rainer," she'd say, "you don't need me anymore. Everybody knows who you are, you've got plenty of supporters, they're very loyal to you, so I don't think you need me anymore."

Maybe she was hoping her comments would spur me to change, but that wasn't going to happen. I cared about her and still do, but I guess the truth is, I cared about my streak more. She gradually came to visit less and less, until eventually our relationship fizzled to nothing. "When I'm the most important thing in your life," she said, "call me."

I never intended to alienate people I cared about, but when I set goals, I do everything I can to achieve them. I've been that way my whole life. It's probably the German in me.

This is not to say I didn't understand the opportunity costs of my streak. If anything, they reinforced my rationale and priorities, however painful it was to stay strong and keep skiing when life went haywire for others around me. Year 7 was particularly difficult in that regard.

In early December 2009, a dear old friend named Mary Elizabeth Broome died in a one-car wreck near Mexican Hat, Utah. She drove off the road and rolled her car multiple times, crushing the driver's side roof and killing her and her dog, Precious. Mary used to wait tables at Barkley's and at the Claimjumper in Frisco. She was into motorcycles and snowmobiles and just lit up the day wherever she was. She was one of the world's beautiful people.

I didn't hear about her death for a few days, but when I did, I stopped to say a prayer for her at the top of the Storm King lift at Copper, first thing in the morning on a bluebird day.

A month later, I found out one of the great friends in my life, Jerry Scholl, was on his deathbed. Jerry and I worked together at Copper many years ago; he taught me quite a bit about moving earth (he built golf courses in the summer) and grooming snow. We called him Bugaloo and Lex Luthor. I knew he was sick, but when I heard that he was near death, I drove to his house to see him once more.

He was only about 50 but he looked like he was 80. His hands were still really big, but all the muscular structure in his body was gone. It broke my heart to see him like that. I lost about five minutes talking to him because I was crying. He didn't need to see more sorrow, so I brought up some of the good times I had with him and all the stuff we'd done together.

Among other things, we reminisced about the days before the resort installed track-it graphs on our cats to monitor us during our shifts. In the spring, the snow goes through a two-hour period every day when it's changing from slush to ice and setting up, and it's useless to groom while that's happening. It just looks like ice cubes. So instead of wasting our time, we would park our cats and play cribbage while the snow did its thing, then once it had set up, we'd go back to work and finish grooming. When they started tracking our RPMs, our two-hour breaks ended and we were left to waste diesel fuel driving around, acting like we were grooming even though you could run over the snow 30 times and it still looked like shit. Jerry and I got some good laughs out of those memories.

He and I had also gone on vacation to Florida; we hit Disney World and Universal Studios, toured Cape Canaveral and the NASA space museum then took a boat out to the Bahamas. We were standing waist deep in the ocean flying my kite as a group of stingrays swam around our ankles. It was a wild experience. We never did get to dive together, which is sad, but that's how life pans out sometimes.

Sitting in a chair next to Jerry's bed was cathartic and crushing at the same time. I rarely got to attend funerals or pay my last respects in person when people died during my streak, simply because logistics wouldn't allow it. But I did with Jerry. One of the last things I said to him was, "When you get up there, Jerry, I want deep powder, blue-sky days, and the greenest greens. I'll see you there."

He nodded and said, "Got it. Deep powder, blue-sky days, and the greenest greens." That was the last thing he said to me.

Less than a month later, in mid-February 2010, another old friend died. Kurt Oliver had been a ski instructor at Hidden Valley when I was in high school; he also rose through the ranks of the National Park Service to become East District ranger of Rocky Mountain National Park. He died of cancer at 61, still living in Estes. I hadn't seen him for a long time, but I respected him a lot and admired his zest for living in the mountains. I paid tribute to him alone at the top of Copper Mountain, remembering him for the man he was when I was a kid. (The following winter, two more friends died: "Air Dale" Scott, another close buddy whom I used to operate lifts with, passed away in his sleep; and Leif Borgeson, who went from patrolling at Copper to directing A-Basin's snow safety program, had a heart attack while hiking a mountain in Aspen with his son.)

That May, as the snow melted into the rivers and A-Basin staged its annual pond-skimming show on Lake Reveal, I watched kids who looked like I once did, full of energy and youth and reckless abandon, schussing across the frigid lake until their speed waned and they went from skimmers to swimmers. Inevitably, they popped up smiling and gasping, fully alive from the rush.

I kept that image in mind as I continued on. Up to Oregon for the summer. A night run under a billion stars with my buddy Jim Bob, then another flight to South America. A month of rambling in Chile as "el Gringo de Guinness."

It wasn't often that I met someone who could relate to my pursuit, but on October 10, 2010 (10/10/10!), I bumped into

Canadian ski mountaineer Greg Hill in Chile. Hill, who lives in Revelstoke, British Columbia, was in the middle of his own world-record ski adventure, trying to climb and ski 2 million vertical feet in one year, all under his own power. We chatted at the bottom of Nevados de Chillan, took a photo together, then went our separate ways to continue our pursuits alone.

    I flew home to Colorado five days later. Due to a dry fall, the only snow available to ski was a 110-foot shot in a stand of north-facing trees at A-Basin. After that, Copper's snowmakers let me ski their piles at the top of the mountain. I did that every day for a week — up and down, up and down — waiting for winter like the rest of the ski bums.

XI

How do you prove that you ski every day? If you don't have a parrot sitting on your shoulder with a point-of-view camera and a real-time video feed, it's not as easy as it sounds. Nor is it easy to track how much you ski, which in my case was crucial. When I started in November 2003, the only way to prove that I'd skied was to check my season-pass scans, and those only chronicled my resort days. I bought an Avocet watch to track my vertical, but it stopped counting after 300,000 feet and you couldn't download the data onto a computer. Everything was handwritten. I put a little tick on a piece of paper every time I got to 300,000 feet and had to reset the watch. I also recorded the number of runs I skied every day.

It wasn't until September 2004, nearly one year after my streak began, that I bought a Suunto watch with the power to download my data onto a computer. This came in handy for recording what I'd done, and it was also just cool to look at. I learned what my pace could be at all the different resorts. For example, I averaged about 7,500 feet per hour at Loveland if I rode Chair 1, 7,300 at A-Basin on Pali, and 7,000 on the Andes Express at Valle Nevado. The best lift that I rode regularly was the Super Bee at Copper. I averaged 10,000 feet an hour on that chair; you ski 2,350 feet every run. The only one that was better was Keystone's Santiago Express. I did about 11,000 feet an hour on Santiago, but I almost never skied Keystone.

In addition to the data I tracked with my watch, I kept daily logs to record whatever stood out from my ski day. Sometimes it was a particular run. Other times it was someone I skied with or a conversation we had. Here was an example from a spring day at A-Basin during Year 8:

I had a bit of a disaster when some people playing with their dog threw a Frisbee right in front of me. The dog, going to the right, me skiing to the left, dog turns around, and everything I could do, doggy got a ski boot in the head. Since today was a beer fest, I didn't stop and apologize, as I may have been pummeled by a bunch of drunks. I hope the dog is OK.

Later that year, I wrote about another wildlife sighting on a sunny September afternoon at Valle Nevado:

Near the end of the day, I saw what I call a snow falcon glide over my chair at the top of the Andes Express. I believe this is one of the birds that I see each spring here. Once the ski area closes, I see a mating pair that circles overhead in a way that their shadow circles me as I ski. This has been going on since I first witnessed them mating in 2005. What a great day on the hill.

In general, I downloaded my data every day after I skied. When I was at home, it was easy: I'd sit down in front of my computer while my lunch was cooking, and plug in a cord from my watch. In Oregon it was a bit more complicated. Usually I'd go down to Charlie's, where they had wifi, order lunch and finish my logs while I was eating. Then I'd pack it all up and go to work. My laptop fit well in my motorcycle sidebag, so that's where it lived. The last summer, I rented an apartment in Govy so I did everything there.

I continued my daily download routine until my last year, on July 28, 2011, when Suunto closed the website and I couldn't load my data anymore. I went back to keeping track by hand.

Through it all, my pursuit of 100 million vertical feet never wavered. But I also celebrated plenty of milestones in terms of the number of days I skied. On January 14, 2011, I equaled Cal Ripken's consecutive-games-played record with my 2,632nd straight day of skiing. "My only wish is that I could earn his hourly wage for all that I have done," I wrote in my log that day.

I realize they were completely different pursuits, but to do either, you had to have the dedication and will and know-how to keep going. For me, skiing through injuries was excruciating; and I know Ripken had to play through some injuries that were excruciating, too. When I passed his number, I thought, *I even beat Cal Ripken!* But again, if I were making the money he was making, I'd be writing this book on a beach in Hawaii.

A number of people told me I should've hired an agent or publicist to maximize my appeal to sponsors during my streak. My buddy in New Zealand, Ric Georgeson, was adamant about that. He thought I could've been much more famous than I was — an internationally known adventurer with corporate backing. But I was always so busy trying to hit my daily numbers then feed myself and make it to work on time that I never put that effort in. I also didn't want to spend money on an agent since I was already so tight on funds as it was. Because of that, Ric said my "trials and tribulations have all been for a private world record." Maybe he was right. I didn't care either way.

On the other hand, I did get free skis from K2 and Voile and outerwear from Spyder, and a number of friends and family supported me financially in their own little ways. For example, my buddy Jim Bob used to either ride my motorcycle back to Colorado when I flew from Oregon to South America, or, if he couldn't do it, he'd pay someone else to do it. He'd cover their gas and meals and a couple of nights' lodging on the way down, then get them a plane ticket back to Oregon after they delivered the bike to Copper. That was his version of sponsorship.

I'm sure in the long run it would've paid to hire a publicist, but it never was about the pay or the fame. It was about challenging myself to see what I could accomplish. Sponsorship would've made life scoochier, but I wouldn't have felt like I did it on my own. And I took great pride in doing it on my own.

Five days after I passed Cal Ripken's number, I dodged a

bullet. While skiing at Copper, the little wire leash that keeps my ski attached to my boot in case I fall and eject from my binding, somehow detached from my boot while I rode the Timberline Express. I never noticed it and took off skiing down a beginner run to the next lift. I was having a grand old time, picking up speed, when all of a sudden the leash slipped under my ski, stopping it cold. It threw me down so hard I thought I broke my leg (I got it X-rayed the next day but they didn't find a fracture). Instead, I had severely hyperextended a ligament. I tried getting it massaged to alleviate the pain, to no avail. And because it was my right leg, it did all the work in my cat and never got a rest. The pain throbbed every day for the rest of my streak.

The snagged leash wasn't the only close call I escaped in Year 8. While at Mt. Hood that summer, I finished a work shift around 1 a.m. and was driving back down the mountain to the apartment I was renting. There was a cliff face on the left side of the road and a dropoff to my right. I came around a corner and all of the sudden a deer landed on the road right in front of me. I grew up in an area where there are deer and elk all over the place, and I've been riding my motorcycle at night since I was old enough to ride. So I know to watch for the little reflector that's out of place.

This time, the deer got so freaked out by my bike that it stopped in its tracks, just like you'd expect a deer in the headlights to do. I grabbed both brakes as hard as I could at 40 mph, and when I stopped my front tire came to rest next to the deer's ribs. The deer ran off immediately, but it took me a few minutes to collect myself. I looked at the cliff, and there was one little slot in the rocks where the deer could come down; that's why I didn't see it until it was on the road. My hands were still shaking when I got home.

I also had to deal with annoying animals from my own species. I guess because I stuck to such a rigid routine on the hill, lapping the same lifts for hours on end, I stood out to the ski patrollers at Timberline. Maybe they resented me because I got to ski all day and they had to lead their boring existence of sitting at the top of the mountain waiting to be needed. While the lifties used to throw me their extra hot dogs as an attaboy gesture of encouragement, some of the patrollers poured lines of salt across the trails to piss off the snowboarders who jibbed off their bamboo poles, snapping the poles by the hundreds each week. They thought they were getting back at the jibbers (we use salt to harden the snow in the summertime), but it affected all of us. When my skis hit a line of salt two inches high and four inches wide, it stopped me like I'd hit a patch of gravel. And they'd often stagger the salt lines so that just when you caught your balance from the first one, you'd hit the second one and lunge forward again.

    I crashed numerous times from the salt, including once when I nearly slid into a field of lava rocks. I stopped at the edge of the snow, right before a dropoff. If I'd hit the lava at the speed I was skiing, I could've died — that's not exaggerating at all. Two other times I crashed so hard just before I flew to Chile that I started my vacation in the Andes with bruised ribs. If the patrollers saw me wipe out, they'd go, "Man, that looked like it hurt!" and wait for a response. I'd say, "Oh, my skis just stopped." I wouldn't let on that it hurt or that it pissed me off, because I knew it would only make the little rats feel good about themselves.

    There was one patroller in particular who busted my chops every run, because he got sick of watching me ski by. I called him the Hero Heckler. He'd say dumb shit like, "How many runs is that?" or "Why don't you stop and talk to us?" My laps only took four minutes, and he always had a new smart-ass comment to yell when I skied by. It got to a point where he became the center of attention among the 50 or so people standing at the top of the lift. I wanted to tell him to grow up and shut up, but again, I knew that would only fan the flames. Instead, I just kept skiing.

***

    Most people are in bed at midnight, not driving up the side of a mountain in a $300,000 tank to go skiing. I didn't know it at the time, but when I climbed into Timberline's Prinoth Demo Cat on September 6, 2011, it would be the last night run of my streak. Jim Bob drove the cat, which we called "The Beast," and I was joined in the cabin by my friend Ellis — a bartender at Charlie's who saw some combat as a Marine before becoming a ski bum — and a little hottie named Caitlin. It was Caitlin's second year joining me for the night run. She used to tease me, "You could be my uncle!" but I wasn't afraid. "So?" I'd say. "I'm experienced!" You never know if the young ones want you or not.

Aside from confirming a driver to take the cat back down the mountain, I rarely made much of an advance plan for my night runs. It was more like: Walk into Charlie's that evening, have a couple of cocktails, and see if anyone wanted to go skiing after midnight.

One night I agreed to take along a ski patroller whom everyone called "The Dude." He was a black guy who partied a little too much, and he was leaving town the next day. When we got to the top of the Palmer Snowfield, he forgot that he'd completely ramped down the DIN on his bindings. He was trying to show me how fast he could crank tight turns, but he kept ejecting out of his bindings and landing in a pile on the snow. After six tumbles, I got sick of picking him up and collecting his skis, so I finally told him, "Look, Dude. You're either going to have to walk or you're going to ski so you don't come out of your bindings, because the last thing I want to do is hike all the way up and get a toboggan and drag your ass down the hill. I'm not messing around. I didn't come up here to babysit. I invited you along because you told me you were a good skier, and that's what I'm expecting."

He was pretty embarrassed, but I made myself clear: "I don't want to spend all night up here. The bar is still open. We can make it."

Another night I had to rescue a snowcat that a female groomer nearly drove off a cliff. She had taken it down the wrong trail and began sliding just above the rock face on a run called Far East. She called for help, which that night meant me. I knew Far East well so I drove down and picked her up in my cat, then dropped her off at the base. Then I went home and put my ski gear on, hitched a ride back to the top of the mountain, skied my last run of the season down Far East, got into her cat and slithered through an old cut in the woods back to safety. It was as sketchy as grooming gets.

The conditions varied for my night runs. There were times when I could barely see 50 feet because it was so cloudy. Other nights, we skied under the bright glow of a full moon. In lean years we sidestepped over barren patches of dirt, scratching up our ski bases. But most of the time the surface was ample and smooth. That was the benefit of driving up in a cat instead of a snowmobile (which I did a few years). You had two cat widths of perfect corduroy to carve on the descent, instead of refrozen coral reef.

For the grand finale in 2011, after hopping out of the cat at 8,500 feet elevation and giving Jim Bob plenty of time to groom the slope back down to the lodge, we started skiing at 12:30 a.m. We descended 2,600 feet — half a vertical mile — then walked into Charlie's just in time to cap the season with a shot of Crown.

***

I stayed in South America until October 16 that year, then flew home to Denver. It was a weak beginning to a weak winter in Colorado, enough to make the "white strip of death" that everyone skis during the early season feel like a tired place to be. Still, I pushed on. On Halloween, I skied 57 runs at A-Basin, cementing my eighth year of daily skiing with 47,523 vertical feet.

The monotony started to get to me after a while, and because so many jonesers were concentrated on such limited terrain, it became harder to hit my numbers. (Who would expect that I, of all people, didn't have enough time to ski?) Complicating matters, we were short staffed to start the season at Copper, so I worked my first grooming shift three weeks before my scheduled start date. I continued putting in long hours, and after about a month and a half, I realized I wasn't hitting my numbers and was falling behind the million-a-month pace. I hated that. I was only three months away from the 100-month date, my Slush Fund was long gone, and there was no way I was going to hit 100 million feet — my ultimate goal — if I kept my job. So I took a deep breath one day, walked into the shop, and gave my boss two weeks' notice. I told him I had to take a sabbatical. I'd worked too hard for too long to come up just short, simply to maintain a paycheck.

And so, from early December 2011 onward, my only job was feeding my streak. I skied six hours a day, sometimes more. Between December 2 and 18, I eclipsed 50,000 vertical feet seven times and hit 45,000 the other nine days. I felt fitter and stronger than I had since my streak began. Even better, I'd gotten myself back on target to hit 100 million feet in 100 months.

Which, of course, is when everything went to shit. I filled up with fluid like a water balloon as my heart fluttered inside me. Yet still I kept skiing. On January 9, I racked up 39,780 vertical feet. I had no idea my life was in danger until I dropped by the Copper Mountain clinic the next morning. Just 49 sunrises shy of the 100-month deadline, I skied 1,444 vertical feet that final day, then checked into the intensive-care unit.

After 2,993 straight days and 98,145,000 vertical feet, my streak was over and I knew it.

Plenty of people had their opinions about my obsession. Some of them worried I was lonely, stuck in this solitary existence that revolved around a solitary pursuit. But it was easy to forget that I'd worked eight hours a day by myself for 30 years. Skiing was my social time.

Most people rarely talk about the deeper parts of life: happiness, fulfillment, why we live the way we do. But I had those conversations several times a day, neatly packaged into the time it takes to ride a chairlift from the bottom of the hill to the top. So, no, I never felt alone.

By the end of my streak, I was beholden to no one — not a wife, not kids, not a boss. Ironically, I belonged instead to a cockamamie adventure, contrived entirely by me. Sure, I was heartbroken when it ended, but in a strange way, that episode validated my entire odyssey. You never know when your life is going to change forever, or end. Might as well seize the days you have.

All along I subscribed to this ideal of being true to myself. There's a fine line between that ideal and selfishness, and I'm not sure where the line exists. But if you don't live for yourself, no one else is going to. Don't believe me? Try it. Pick something you want to do, and do it. No excuses.

I wanted to ski every day, so I skied every day. It was as simple as that.

EPILOGUE

What happens when your purpose ends? This was the question I faced in the wake of my streak. I designed my life to support my daily skiing. Once my streak ended and I hit 100 million vertical feet, I essentially had to redesign my life.

You might be surprised to learn I no longer ski every day, even in the winter. I go out on good days, when the snow is soft and the wind isn't raking the skin off my nose, but it feels pretty good to not *have* to ski.

As I write this epilogue nearly three years after my heart arrhythmia ended my streak, I still live at the base of Copper Mountain and I still groom snow for the resort. This winter will be my 33rd straight winter working for Copper. But instead of following the snow around the world, I stick around during the summer. I go touring on my motorcycle. Last year I bought a bike in Hawaii and stored it with some friends on the Big Island, to be ridden whenever I head down that way. I'm keeping my eye out for a sailboat, too.

Based on a conservative estimate, I figure I skied about 928,000 miles during my streak — enough to circumnavigate the planet 37 times or travel to and from the moon three and a half times. In addition to the 16 pairs of skis I went through, my streak wore out four computers and three altimeter watches.

I wish I could say it left me healthier than before I started, but that part is up for debate. The year after my heart started fluttering, I broke my leg racing a NASTAR course. Then, last September, during a long off-road motorcycle tour outside Moab, Utah, I got bucked off my bike and severely injured a tendon in my ankle. Thankfully my bike stopped just shy of landing on top of me; if it had, with how hot the engine was and how remote my location was at the time, I might not be here to finish this story. I spent that night curled up in a ball on the dirt road, shivering in my riding gear, hoping I might see someone who could help me. It wasn't until the next day that I finally got out and found a tow truck to extricate the bike.

When I got my ankle checked out, the doctors noticed that one of the toes on my other foot was badly infected — and probably had been for a while. They had no choice but to amputate part of it. I blame that on the streak. For how many days I kept my feet in ski boots for eight hours and how many nights I was too tired to do anything but collapse in my tent and go to sleep, it's no surprise I am now living with only 9 ½ toes. I feel fortunate that the rest of me is intact.

You might be wondering what ever happened with Guinness. I will spare you the full breadth of my disgust and leave it at this: After they created a category for most vertical feet skied on consecutive days on telemark gear — tailored to my streak — they gave me a Claim Number and requested I send them everything I had to prove what I'd done. I spent $300 on postage to get them what they asked for. Lo and behold, shortly after I did this, they changed their mind, deleted the category, and informed me that I should instead try to break the record for most vertical skied over 24 hours.

So my streak is not in the Guinness Book of World Records and probably never will be. I had a hard time getting past that at first. Even though I was never in it for recognition, for some reason making it into the record book seemed like a fair token of validation for all that I did.

As time passed, however, I realized that holding an "official world record" would only be for others. I did this for me — how it made me feel, the purpose it gave me, the experiences I had.

I never did get rich, but skiing sure made me happy.

—Rainer Hertrich, August 2015

ACKNOWLEDGMENTS

Countless people and places combined to make my streak and this book a reality. First and foremost, thank you, Mom and Dad, for allowing me to live. In addition, Peter, may he rest in peace, was a huge supporter, and my Uncle Adolf and Aunt Gabbi provided invaluable inspiration to continue on.

Being the groovy groomer/snowmaker/ski bum that I am, I would like to thank Mother Earth for providing the terrain and weather that make it all possible. Without the snow and mountains, nothing else matters.

Copper Mountain will always be my favorite resort of the dozens that I was privileged to ski. Next on that list would be Timberline Lodge at Mt. Hood, Oregon. What a great crew. I'm grateful for the training that Jake and Jason had at Copper and the fact that Buzzard was friends with Cruiser, which got me in the door. And I remain eternally indebted to Jeff Flood, a.k.a. "Flood-o," who gave me the opportunity to groom there.

So many friends and staff helped keep me going in dire circumstances. On days when the weather was so horrid that none of the lifts or terrain opened, I got lucky and met up with people who were headed up the hill for maintenance purposes and gave me a ride to ski. Same goes for all the anonymous angels who picked me up on the side of the road in Chile. Muchas gracias!

An enormous thanks to my family and friends who recognized my commitment and excused me from events and milestone celebrations to let me pursue my dream. You supported me in so many ways that it would take another book to even start to describe them.

To K2, Voile, Spyder, my dear friend Fuxi, Leki, Telemark Down, Oakley, Scott, Smith, Gordini, Black Diamond, and all the BMW motorcycle shops around North America that worked on my bike: Thank you from the bottom of my heart for keeping my engine running, both figuratively and literally.

I am grateful to Devon O'Neil for his enthusiasm, motivation, support, and insight that made this book happen.

If there is anyone I haven't mentioned — and I know there are! — thank you also. The love I felt throughout this streak was invaluable.

I hope you enjoyed the read as much as I enjoyed all the people and places I met along the way.

CREDITS

Jacket design: Nikki LaRochelle

Cover photo: Rainer Hertrich at Copper Mountain, by Marc Piscotty

Back cover photo: Rainer Hertrich at Mt. Hood, by Daniel Root

Coauthor Devon O'Neil is a freelance journalist in Breckenridge, Colorado. His work appears regularly in *Outside*, *SKI*, *Powder*, and *Backcountry* magazines, as well as on ESPN.com.

www.ingramcontent.com/pod-product-compliance
Lightning Source LLC
Chambersburg PA
CBHW071314110426
42743CB00042B/1996